Sami Alwani

The Pleasure of the Text

Contents

SAEHMEH THE DOG
IN: "the Misfortunes of Virtue"

"A DESPAIRING ADULT DOG ART COMIC/DISCONTINUOUS MONTAGE (...) THE PERFECTION OF A FALSE DIALECTIC OF SUFFERING" "WHEN YOU DESIRE CONTROL YOU LET DESIRE CONTROL YOU"

10:30 AM
ONE DAY I'LL ESCAPE
I'M REALLY GONNA TRY MY HARDEST, YOU GUYS

11:00
RT SUPPLY
AH
TO BEGIN AGAIN, WITHOUT RESTING
AS LONG AS I CAN CONTINUE TO PROJECT MY EXTRADIEGETIC PSEUDO-MYSTICAL NARRATIVE (INCESSANT ORGANIZATION AND RECOMBINATION OF FORMS, ASSOCIATIONS) OVERTOP THIS OPPRESSIVELY RATIONAL LIVED EXPERIENCE...
... I CAN KEEP MYSELF FROM CHOKING ON THE SUFFOCATING OBEISANCE TO MATERIALISM WHICH SURROUNDS ME
"THIS IS ALL A DREAM"
"SOME FANTASTICAL GAME"
"HAHA"
3:00
ON GRINDR
FOR OLDER 26
FOR OLDER 26
INTELLIGENT, EDUCATED YOUNGER DOG SEEKING ATTRACTIVE OLDER MAN FOR NON COMMITTED CASUAL/MEANINGFUL INTIMACY
hTC
I LOVE ARAB DOGS
ARABIC DOGS ARE SO HOT
NICE PIC
PHOTO RECIEVED
ARE YOU REALLY ARABIC?

4:00

8:15

THERE IS NO BOTTOM TO THE DEPTHS OF WHICH I WILL NOT SINK...

* CHURLISH DISQUIETING LAUGHTER *

MY ANGUISH IS FOUNDATIONLESS AND ETERNAL

THE SPIRITUAL MALNOURISHMENT OF CITY LIFE IS SO DELICIOUSLY ENTERTAINING
LIKE A MANY-FACED DEMON WHOSE ESSENCE CHANGES DEPENDING ON THE ANGLE AT WHICH HE'S VIEWED
AND THE LONGER I LISTEN TO THIS DEMON'S DESOLATE SOLILOQUIES THE MORE I RECOGNIZE HIS VOICE AS MY OWN
IS IT MYSTICISM? OR PERHAPS A NEUROCHEMICAL IMBALANCE
WHICH ALLOWS ME THROUGH SOME OBSCURE INTERNAL MECHANISM TO TRANSFORM MY MISERY... INTO EXUBERANCE...
HOW DROLL- YOU MANUFACTURE THESE EXPERIENCES WITH THE SOLE INTENTION OF AFFIXING AND MINIATURIZING THEM INTO THE BANAL COMEDY OF YOUR ART
PATHETIC
YOU'RE QUITE HOPELESS REALLY!
THANK YOU!!!
I DON'T DESERVE SUCH CHARITY!!
THAT THE SUSPICIONS OF VIOLENCE MY PARA-NOID DELUSIONS HAVE TRAINED ME TO EXPECT FROM A HOSTILE ENVIRONMENT...
...SHOULD FINALLY BE CONFIRMED!!
HONK! HONK!
LATER
IT IS BETTER
ENDURING VIOLENCE IS BETTER THAN THE EXPECTATION OF VIOLENCE

I CAN'T LET THIS NEW GUY KNOW HOW INTO HIM I AM
AND I DEFINITELY CAN'T SHOW HIM MY ART OR HE'LL THINK I'M A BIG CREEP!
I ALSO HAVE TO BE CAREFUL NOT TO MENTION MY ANXIETY DISORDER!
...BECAUSE PEOPLE FIND THAT SORT OF THING ALIENATING!!
I'LL DO MY LAUNDRY TONIGHT SO I CAN WEAR THAT NICE PINK RALPH LAUREN BUTTON DOWN WHEN WE MEET
OH MY GOD! MY SHOWER IS FILTHY! WHAT IF HE WANTS TO HAVE A SHOWER AFTER WE HAVE SEX!!
I SHOULD NOT ASSUME WE'RE GOING TO HAVE SEX!
BUT PROBABLY WE WILL!
ON A DATE!
SEMIOTICS IS THE STUDY OF SIGNS AND SYMBOLS...
SOMEONE WHO STUDIES SEMIOTICS IS CALLED A SEMIOTICIAN
WELL THEN I GUESS I'M A "SAEHMEH-OTICIAN..."
HAHA

BJ in the Park!
CELEBRATING MY GAY HERITAGE!
AWOOOOO!!

EVERY NIGHT I TOIL AT MY DRAFTING TABLE

HOURS UPON HOURS...
DAYS UPON DAYS...

THE PURITY OF MY VISION WILL LEND ME THE WINGS I CAN USE TO TRANSCEND THIS PROSAIC REALITY
POST

VICE
BURN THE MANUSCRIPT!
NO! HE'S JUST A FUCKING DOG!!
SLAM!
THE NEW YORK TIMES
MAKE SURE HE NEVER REALIZES HOW TALENTED AN ARTIST HE REALLY IS ...
FANTAGRAPHICS
WOW!! THIS GUY'S REALLY GOOD AT DRAWING!
TOO BAD HE'S ONLY A DOG...

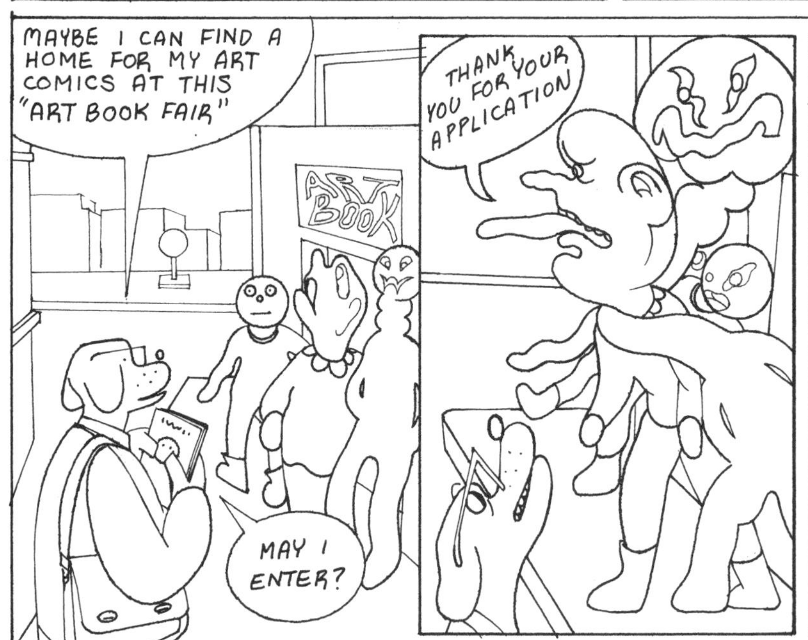
MAYBE I CAN FIND A HOME FOR MY ART COMICS AT THIS "ART BOOK FAIR"
ART BOOK
MAY I ENTER?
THANK YOU FOR YOUR APPLICATION

UNFORTUNATELY, DUE TO THE HIGH VOLUME OF SUBMISSIONS WE ARE NOT ABLE TO OFFER YOU A SPOT AT THIS TIME
AH!
YOU'VE BEEN ADDED TO OUR WAITLIST, WE WILL NOTIFY YOU IF ANYTHING BECOMES AVAILABLE

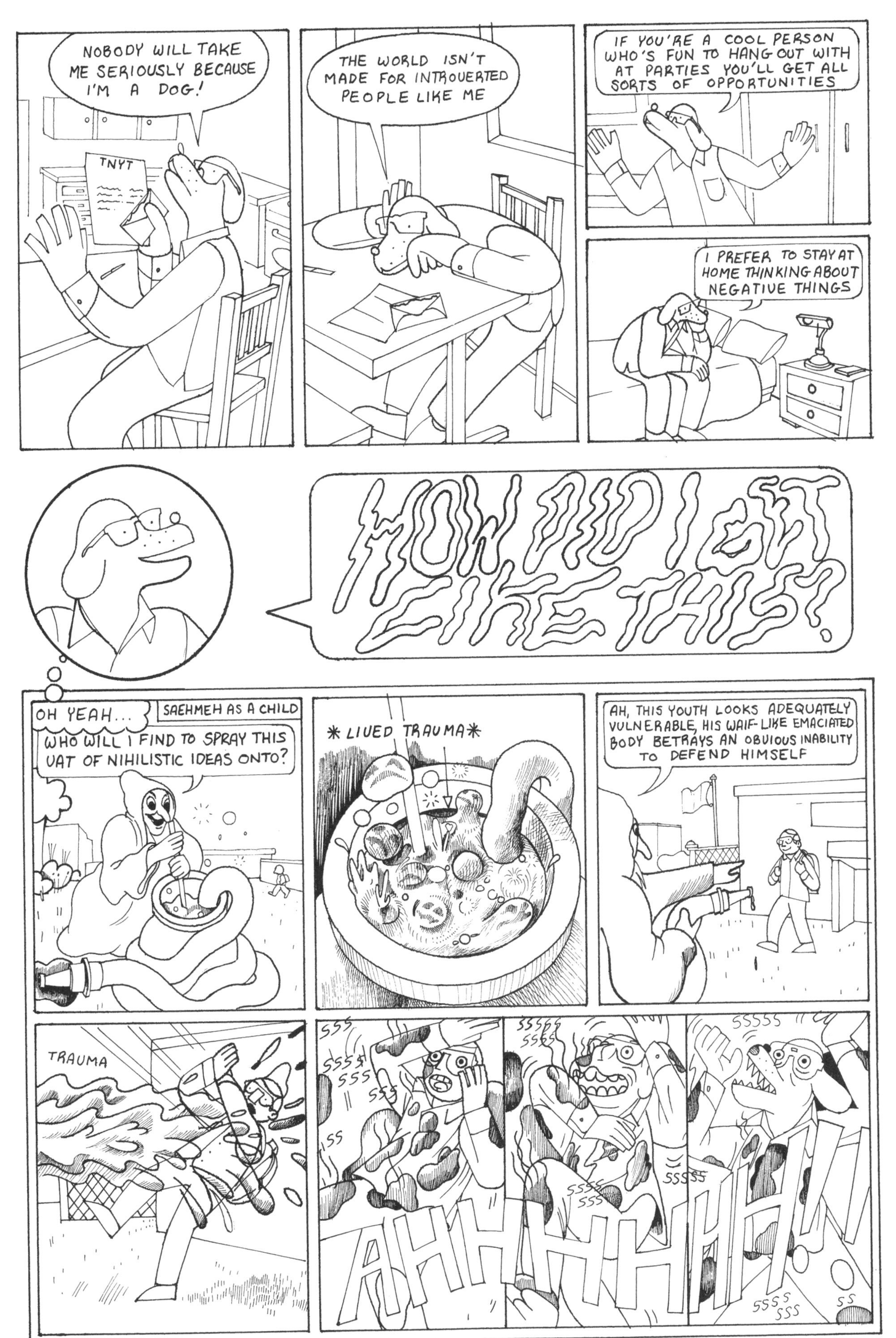
NOBODY WILL TAKE ME SERIOUSLY BECAUSE I'M A DOG!
TNYT
THE WORLD ISN'T MADE FOR INTROVERTED PEOPLE LIKE ME
IF YOU'RE A COOL PERSON WHO'S FUN TO HANG OUT WITH AT PARTIES YOU'LL GET ALL SORTS OF OPPORTUNITIES
I PREFER TO STAY AT HOME THINKING ABOUT NEGATIVE THINGS
HOW DID I GET LIKE THIS?
OH YEAH...
SAEHMEH AS A CHILD
WHO WILL I FIND TO SPRAY THIS VAT OF NIHILISTIC IDEAS ONTO?
* LIVED TRAUMA *
AH, THIS YOUTH LOOKS ADEQUATELY VULNERABLE, HIS WAIF-LIKE EMACIATED BODY BETRAYS AN OBVIOUS INABILITY TO DEFEND HIMSELF
TRAUMA
AHHHHHH!!

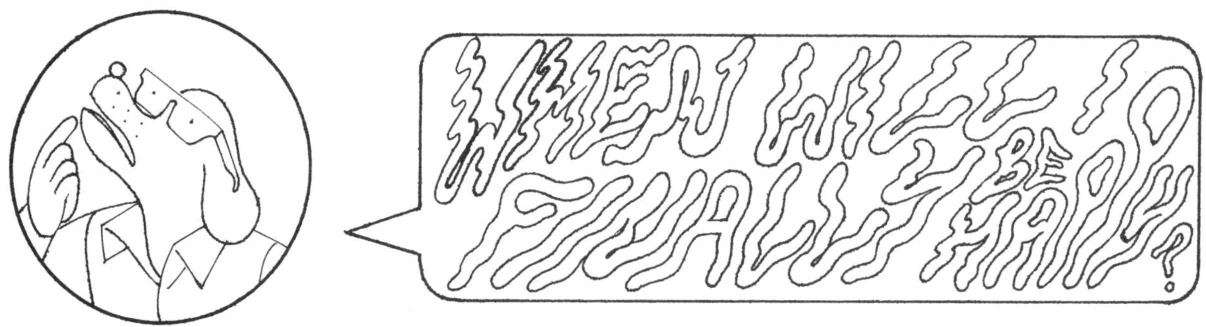
WHEN WILL I BE FINALLY HAPPY?

FINALLY, THROUGH MY WIDELY DISTRIBUTED INDEPENDENT ART COMICS I HAVE MANAGED TO ABOLISH CAPITALISM, RACISM, MISOGYNY, HOMOPHOBIA AND TRANSPHOBIA
BENEVOLENT MACHINES HAVE ELIMINATED ALL JOBS, ALLOWING HUMANS TO SURVIVE ON A UNIVERSAL BASIC INCOME AND PURSUE THE FULFILLMENT OF THEIR HIGHEST FACULTIES
THERE IS NO MORE OPPRESSION OR INJUSTICE IN THE WORLD AND EVERYONE IS FREE
I CAN NOW WHILE AWAY MY DAYS READING OBSCURE PRINTED MATTER, HOSTING MY QPOC FILM SERIES AND THROWING FABULOUS PARTIES ALONGSIDE MY GREGARIOUS, CULTURED, ARTICULATE AND EXCEEDINGLY HANDSOME HUSBAND AND LIFE PARTNER
IN THE MEANTIME SAEHMEH CONTINUES TO BE HAUNTED BY NIGHT-TERRORS
ZZZZZZZZZZZZ
MUST...
...DESTROY NEOLIBERALISM...
DEREGULATED FREE MARKET CAPITALISM

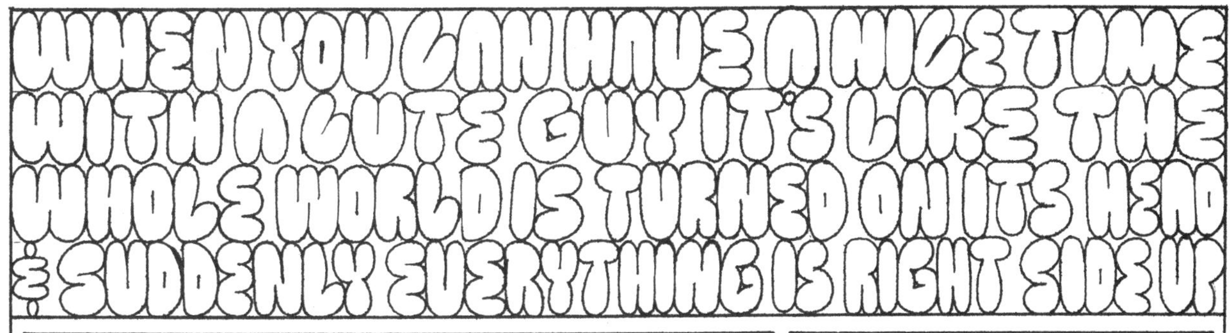
WHEN YOU CAN HAVE A NICE TIME WITH A CUTE GUY IT'S LIKE THE WHOLE WORLD IS TURNED ON ITS HEAD & SUDDENLY EVERYTHING IS RIGHT SIDE UP

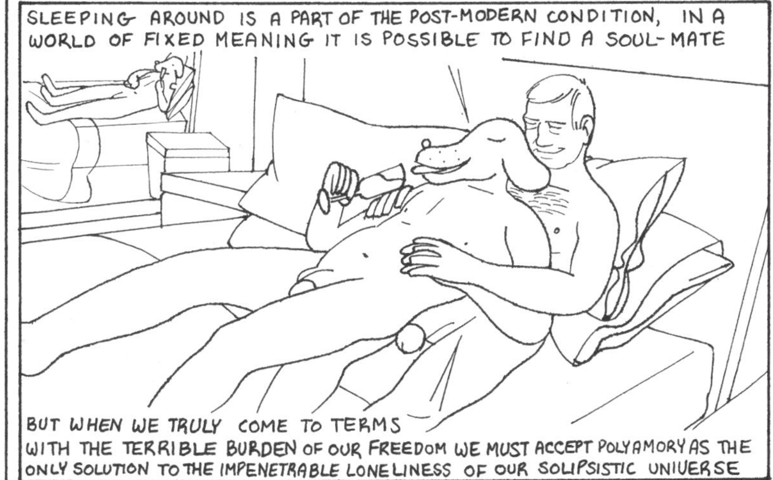
SLEEPING AROUND IS A PART OF THE POST-MODERN CONDITION, IN A WORLD OF FIXED MEANING IT IS POSSIBLE TO FIND A SOUL-MATE
BUT WHEN WE TRULY COME TO TERMS WITH THE TERRIBLE BURDEN OF OUR FREEDOM WE MUST ACCEPT POLYAMORY AS THE ONLY SOLUTION TO THE IMPENETRABLE LONELINESS OF OUR SOLIPSISTIC UNIVERSE

MORE WINE?

I DON'T THINK THE PEN IS WORKING
IT'S LIGHTING UP AT THE END

HERE, BLOW INTO THE LIGHT AND SEE IF YOU GOT ANYTHING

"SOMETIMES LINGERING IN THE TENDERNESS OF YOUR EMBRACE IT FEELS AS IF NOTHING ELSE EXISTS OUTSIDE OF WHAT'S SHARED BETWEEN US"

ONE NIGHT A DERANGED EDITOR, HAVING RECENTLY SUFFERED AN ANEURYSM, FINDS SAEHMEH'S DISCARDED MANUSCRIPT IN THE TRASH BIN AMONG A STACK OF PORNOGRAPHIC MAGAZINES

ARGH!!
AHH!!

BRILLIANT!!
SEX!
TITS!
HOT GIRLS

SAEHMEH'S FIRST PUBLISHED WORK MEETS HIGHLY FAVORABLE REVIEWS
THE BOOK IS TRANSLATED INTO MULTIPLE LANGUAGES AND DISTRIBUTED INTERNATIONALLY
SAEHMEH EXPLODES IN POPULARITY

A PERIOD OF EXTREME PRODUCTIVITY...

SELECTED BIBLIOGRAPHY (2019 - 2023):

"MODERN MAN IN SEARCH OF A SOUL"
FANTAGRAPHICS BOOKS
2019

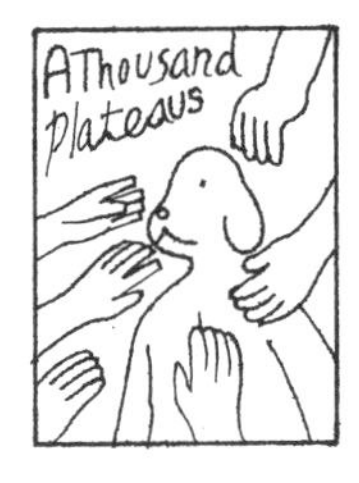

"A THOUSAND PLATEAUS"
HARPER - COLLINS
2020

"THE OWL IN DAYLIGHT"
FARRAR, STRAUSS AND GIROUX
2021

A NUMBER OF CRITICAL SCHOLARLY TEXTS EMERGE ON AEHLAWAHNI'S OEUVRE

"THE TERROR OF BEING: NAVIGATING OTHERNESS & SYSTEMS OF POWER IN THE WORK OF SAEHMEH AEHLAWAHNI"
THIERRY GROENSTEEN - CAMBRIDGE UNIVERSITY PRESS
2021

SEVERAL ARTIST'S MONOGRAPHS

"POST-MODERN CARTOONIST"
PHAIDON PRESS
2023

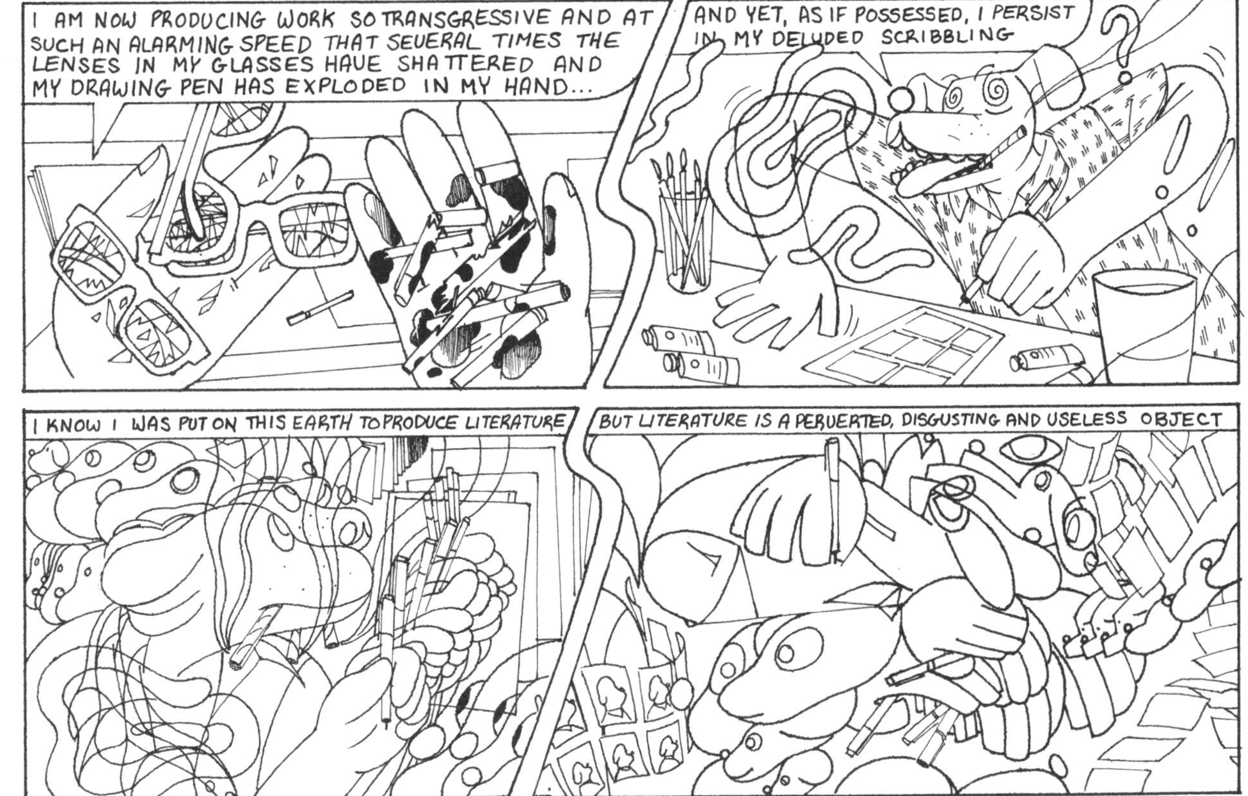

The New York Times
FLEDGLING COMICS SAVANT AEHLAWAHNI BIRTHS YET ANOTHER MASTERPIECE
SUBVERSIVE CANADIAN COMICS FLOURISH AMIDST DILUTE MILQUETOAST OF PROSE LITERATURE
ENFANT TERRIBLE

WHITNEY BIENNIAL

WHERE'S SAEHMEH?
HE'S OVER THERE TALKING SHIT ABOUT THE SCENE AGAIN

HA HA
HAHA
-LAYERING ONE MEANINGLESS AESTHETIC ATOP ANOTHER LIKE SOME IDEOLOGICAL TIRAMISU!!
HAHAHAHA!
HA HA

IS THAT CHARLES SAATCHI??

-GAZING DOWN AT MY NAVEL AS I DISSOLVE INTO A LUKEWARM BATH OF MY OWN REMINISCENCES!!
HAHA HAHA!
HAHAHA HAHAHAHA
HAHAHA!

EXCUSE ME SIR BUT YOU CAN'T SMOKE IN HERE
HAHA!
HA HA
HA HA
HA HAHA!

GRRR!!!

WHAT DO YOU THINK OF THE NEW WORK?
MESMERIZING

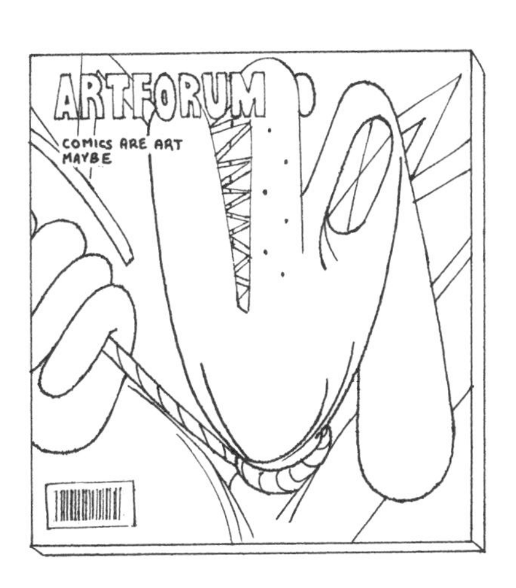
ARTFORUM
COMICS ARE ART MAYBE

TORONTO INTERNATIONAL FILM FESTIVAL
REMIERING TONIGHT: SAEHMEH - A TERRY ZWIGOFF FILM
SOMETIMES I WISH I WASN'T SUCH A BITTER PERSON
BUT THEN I REMEMBER HOW CRUEL AND MISERABLE THIS PLANET REALLY IS
THE SCOPE OF HUMAN HISTORY APPEARS TO ME AS A SINGLE ONGOING ATROCITY
ONLY MY COMICS CAN SALVAGE THESE GLEAMING FRAGMENTS FROM THE WRECKAGE OF HUMAN SUFFERING
THE BEAUTY OF MY SYSTEM IS THAT THE ANGRIER I GET THE MORE I AM MOBILIZED TOWARDS DIRECT ACTION
SAEHMEH'S ESTATE IN MIAMI
THIS HANDSOME SQUIRREL KEEPS HANGING OUT IN OUR BACKYARD

"BEYOND REPROACH"

"SOMETIMES IT FEELS LIKE THE DEVIL IS STALKING ME"

RRARRRGGHHH!!!
DRUNK & DOPED! BELLIGERENT ICONOCLAST SAEHMEH AEHLAWAHNI BURNED ALL BRIDGES WITH THE ALTERNATIVE COMICS COMMUNITY THIS WEEKEND AFTER MAKING A PUBLIC SPECTACLE OF HIMSELF AT THIS YEAR'S SMALL PRESS EXPO!
TMZ
TMZ
A ONCE BRILLIANT FLAME DIMS AS AEHLAWAHNI CONTINUES TO STRUGGLE WITH DRUG ABUSE AND DETERIORATING MENTAL
AEHLAWAHNI REFUSED TO COMMENT WHEN APPROACHED BY TMZ. WE SPOKE WITH HIS FORMER ASSOCIATE
ARGH!
SMASH!!
PANT PANT PANT PANT
POOR DOG
I FEEL SORRY FOR HIM...
HE HAS EVERYTHING BUT WHAT DOES HE REALLY HAVE?

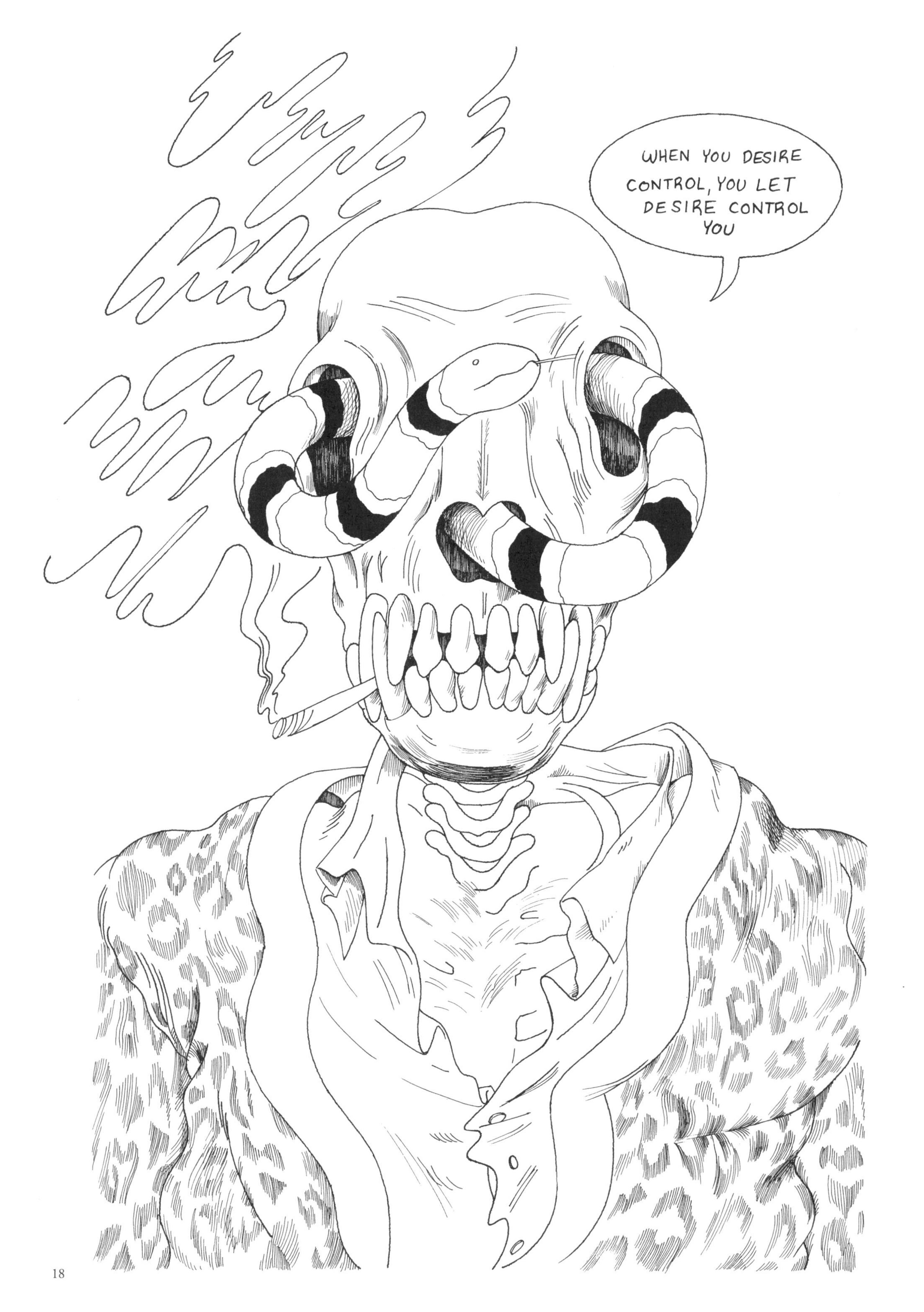
WHEN YOU DESIRE CONTROL, YOU LET DESIRE CONTROL YOU

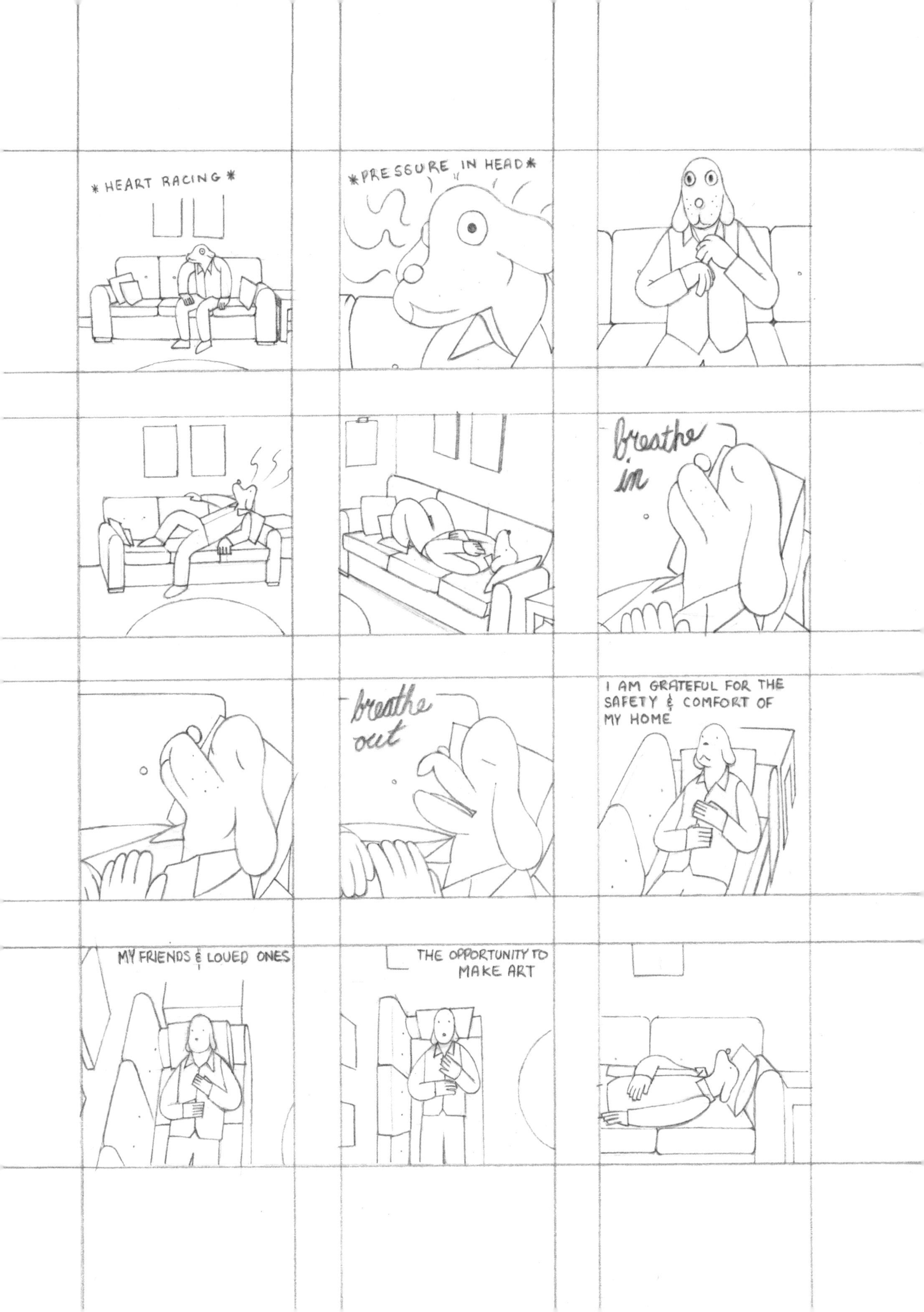
HEART RACING
PRESSURE IN HEAD
breathe in
breathe out
I AM GRATEFUL FOR THE SAFETY & COMFORT OF MY HOME
MY FRIENDS & LOVED ONES
THE OPPORTUNITY TO MAKE ART

SAEHMEH
IN
SAEHMEH AEHLAWAHNI
HAPPY DAYS

IF YOU'RE TRYING TO CONVINCE ME THAT REALITY EXISTS — LET ME JUST WARN YOU
YOU'RE GOING TO HAVE A HARD TIME!

MY STOMACH HURTS. I'VE BEEN SICK FOR SIX DAYS.
BUT I STILL GO TO WORK!

EVERYTHING UNRAVELS & REVEALS IT-SELF TO BE PERFORMANCE —
WHY SHOULD I BE UPSET ?

WHAT IS IT THAT SITS BEHIND MY CONSCIOUSNESS?
I HAVE A SUSPICION THAT IT ISN'T ANYTHING AT ALL

WHEN I GET HOME I'M TOO TIRED TO DO ANYTHING BUT GET HIGH AND JERK OFF

THE MILD & SACCHARINE DEVASTATION OF ORGASM REMINDS ME I'M HUMAN
RAW

THE DISCOURSE OF THE CULTURE I SUBSIST IN SUBSUMES ME

"IT'S YOUR FAULT!! PLASTIC STRAWS!"
"SOME PEOPLE WANT TO GO MISSING!"

A WRAITH SITS ON MY CHEST AS I SLEEP THEN PARTS UPON WAKING
I FEEL REFRESHED
POP!

TIME IS BEING PULLED APART, LIKE AN ELASTIC. I CAN'T FEEL ANYTHING.

UH-OH! SHE'S CAUGHT A WHIFF OF THE DECAYING STENCH OF LEPROSY WHICH LINGERS IN MY BODY!
??

SAEHMEH, YOU'RE NOT OKAY.
WHY DO YOU ASK?!?
UNDER MY SKIN A YAWNING VOID

BURDOCK CAYENNE
COUNTLESS BOTTLES OF COLD-PRESSED JUICE, KOMBUCHA AND BOB MARLEY'S MELLOW MOOD
AM I THAT TRANSPARENT ?

YOU CAN'T HAVE HAPPINESS WITHOUT MISERY, WHY SHOULD MISERY EXIST WITHOUT HAPPINESS?
WHERE DOES ONE BEGIN AND THE OTHER END?

ECSTATIC DEPRESSION
DEPRESSIVE ECSTACY
EXPECTING THIS SATANIC TEXT CASTS A HEX ON ME

I JUST FINISHED WITH ONE DEADLINE AND NOW WORKING TOWARDS ANOTHER.

I NEVER LEAVE MY HOME BECAUSE I AM A DILIGENT WORKER AND LOVE PRODUCING ARTWORK

I ONLY FEEL LONELY WHEN I CONSIDER MY LONELINESS

MOST OF THE TIME I AM NOT AWARE OF ANYTHING
PSD

HAVING SHED MY IDENTITY IN A PROCESS OF SELF-ANNIHILATION THROUGH ART MAKING

AM I OBSESSED WITH POWER & FAME?

OR SIMPLY PARALYZED BY DEBILITATING SOCIAL ANXIETY

IN MY WORK I AM ABLE TO RECONSTRUCT MYSELF ALONG A HIGHER ORDER OF CONSCIOUSNESS

THERE IS A SMALL WINDOW BESIDE MY DRAFTING TABLE

THE VIEW FROM MY *HERMITAGE*

I MERGE WITH MY ENVIRONMENT.

MY ASCETICISM AFFORDS ME THE PLEASURE OF LIMITLESSNESS. A HUMAN ARTIFACT EMBEDDED IN AN INFINITE PROCESSION OF FORMS.

LOOK AT ME!

MY NAME IS SAMI ALWANI

I'M JUST A REGULAR GUY

"I LOVE BEING ENSLAVED"

"CAPITALISM BENEFITS ME SO I DON'T CARE ABOUT THE WELL-BEING OF THOSE IT EXPLOITS"

"I LISTEN TO THE SAME TYPE OF MUSIC EVERYONE ELSE ENJOYS"

BUT WHEN I GET HIGH I TURN INTO AN INSANE MANIAC

"PROPERTY IS THEFT!"

"THERE IS NO ESCAPE FROM THE HELL WE HAVE CREATED FOR OURSELVES"

"HOODRICH PABLO JUAN IS THE GREATEST RAPPER OF ALL TIME"

THERE IS A LEUEL OF ARTISTRY BEYOND MASTERY OF FORM, WHICH IS THE TOTAL PERFECTION OF THE ARTIST'S SOUL

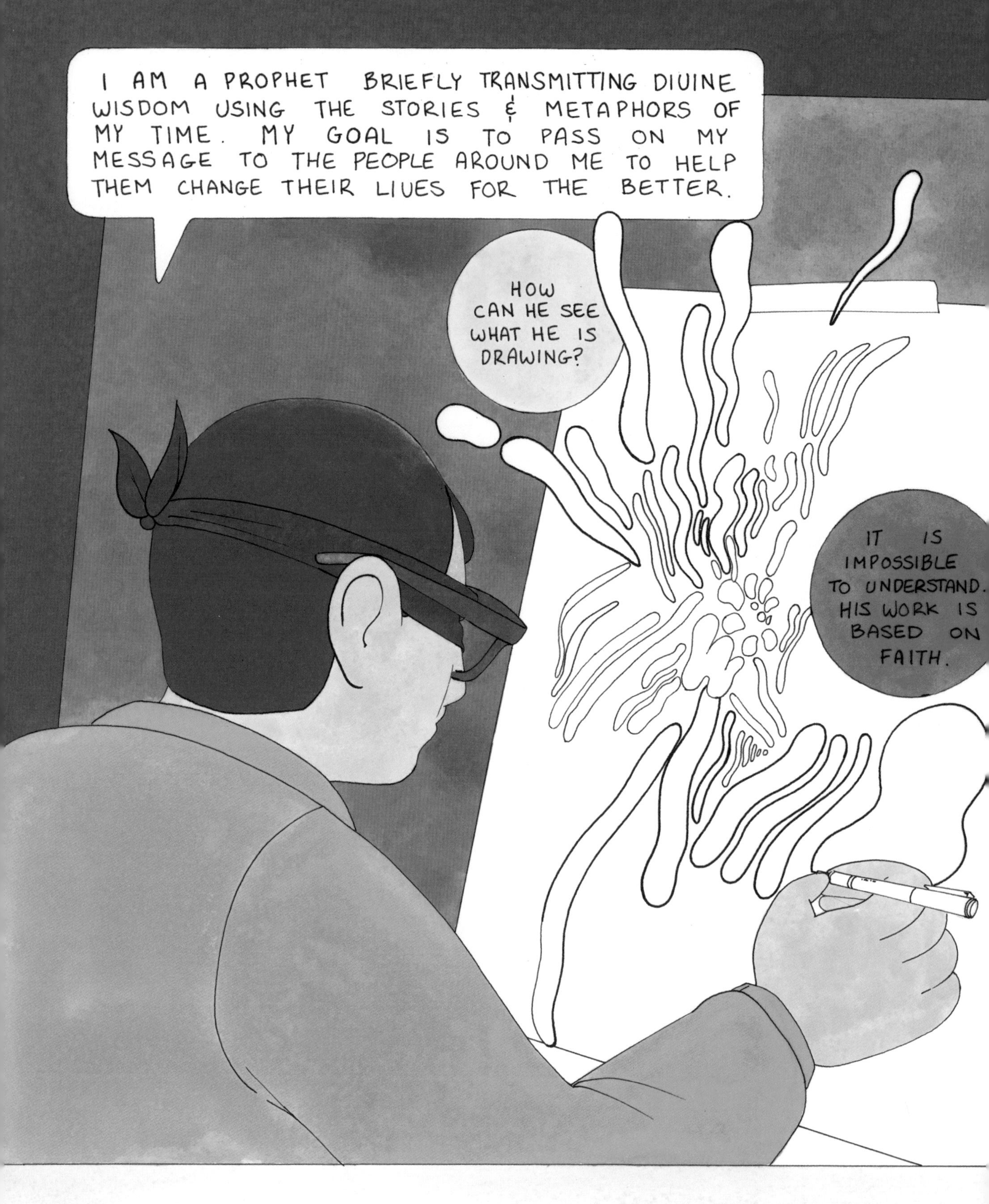

I NEED TO KEEP WRITING WORDS AT ALL COSTS

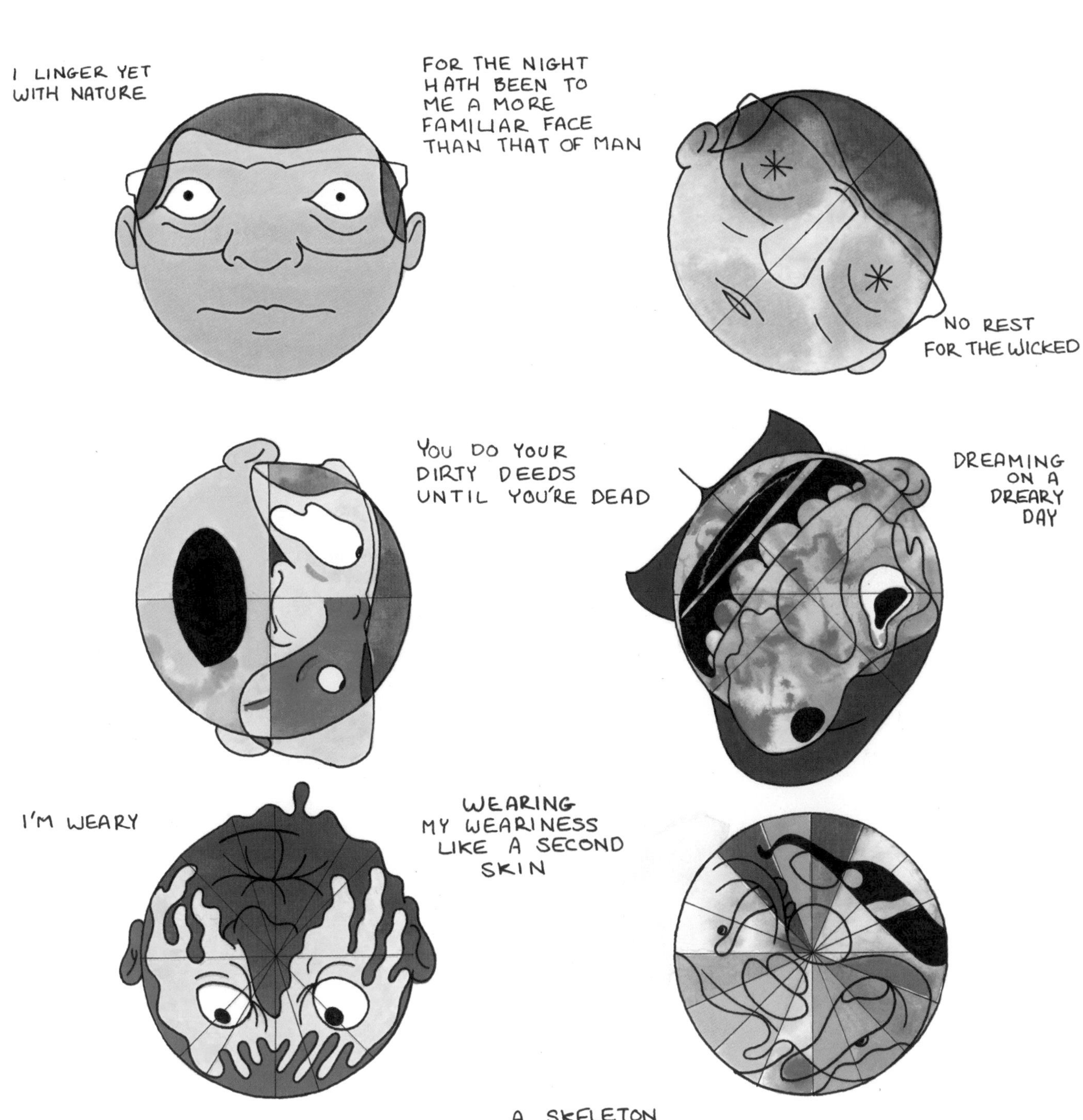
I LINGER YET
WITH NATURE
FOR THE NIGHT
HATH BEEN TO
ME A MORE
FAMILIAR FACE
THAN THAT OF MAN
NO REST
FOR THE WICKED
YOU DO YOUR
DIRTY DEEDS
UNTIL YOU'RE DEAD
DREAMING
ON A
DREARY
DAY
I'M WEARY
WEARING
MY WEARINESS
LIKE A SECOND
SKIN

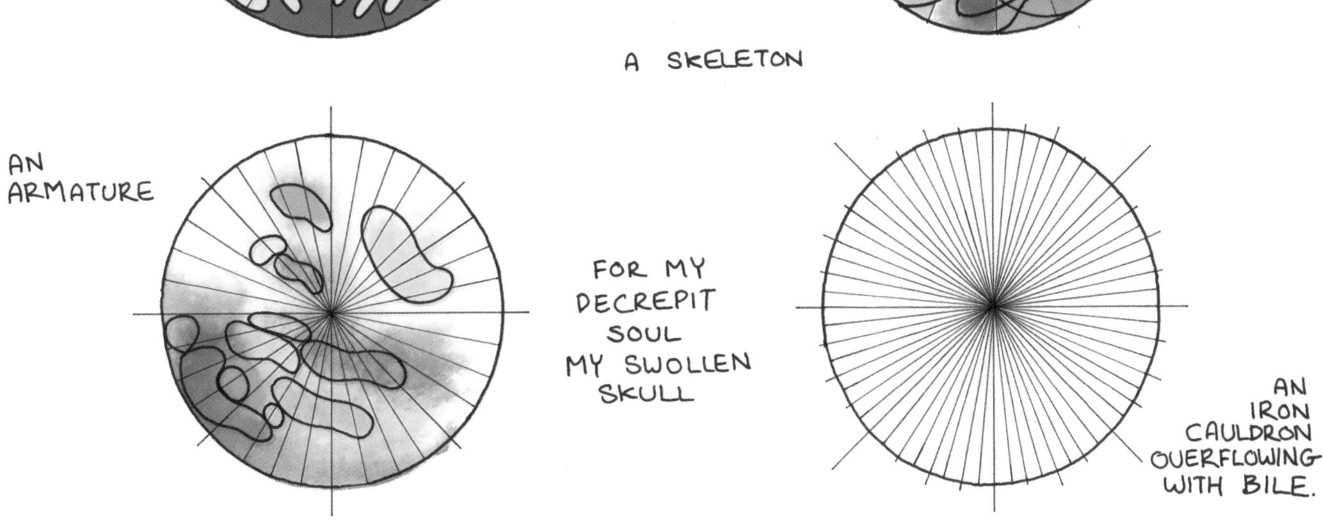
A SKELETON
AN
ARMATURE
FOR MY
DECREPIT
SOUL
MY SWOLLEN
SKULL
AN
IRON
CAULDRON
OVERFLOWING
WITH BILE.

THE IDIOT

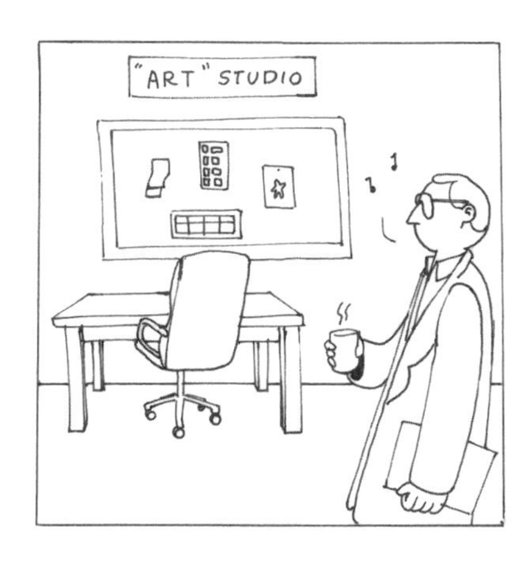
"ART" STUDIO

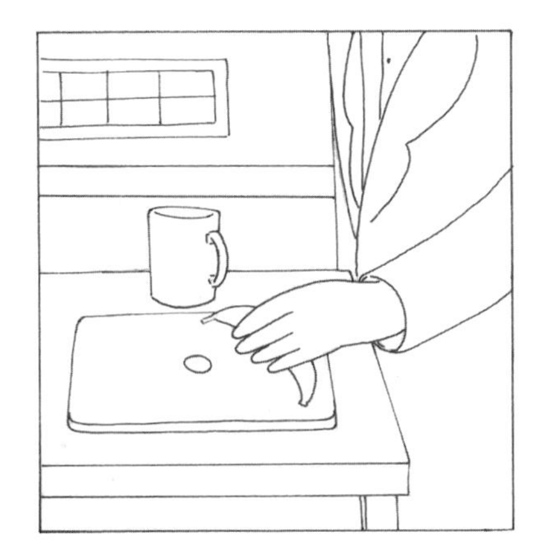

SIGH

OH
HELLO
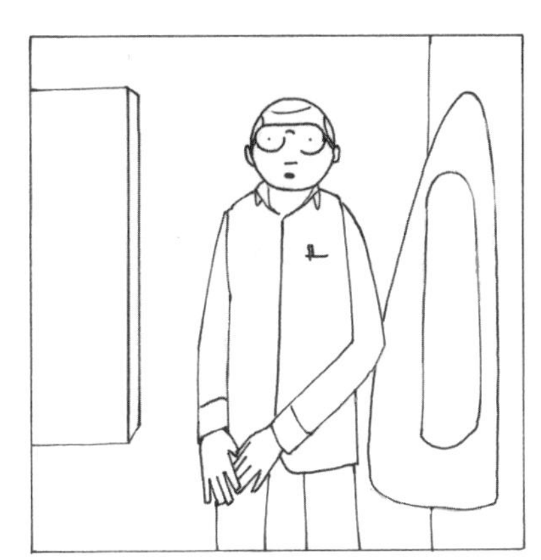

UH...

WELCOME TO MY STUDIO . . .

-WOULD

WOULD YOU LIKE A TOUR?

OKAY-
WELL

THIS- IS MY WRITING CENTRE
ART STUDIO
UH

AND MY PAINT STATION . . .

AND THIS IS THE MAGIC ART MAKING MACHINE
MYSTERY MACHINE

THAT PRODUCES ALL OF MY STORIES
MYSTERY MACHIN

. . .
MYSTERY MACHIN

WHAT IS A STORY, YOU ASK?

WELL
A STORY IS JUST A THEORETICAL CONSTRUCT

WITHOUT ANY INNATE MEANING OR VALUE

JUST LIKE EVERYTHING ELSE WE ENCOUNTER ON EARTH

LET ME SHOW YOU HOW THE MACHINE WORKS
STERY

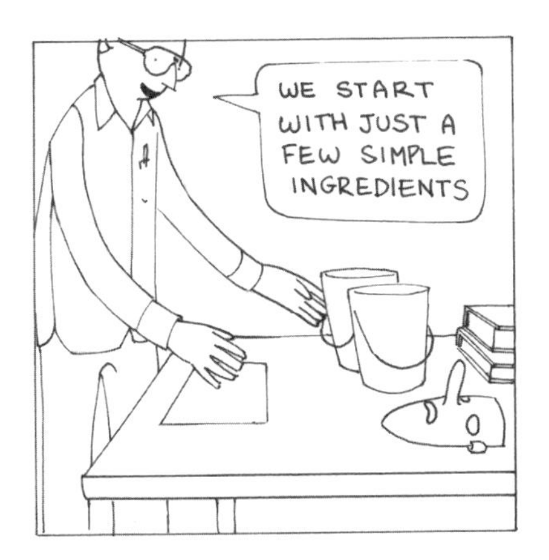
WE START WITH JUST A FEW SIMPLE INGREDIENTS

YSTERY MACHINE
AND POUR THEM INTO THE MACHINE

GRAPHITE

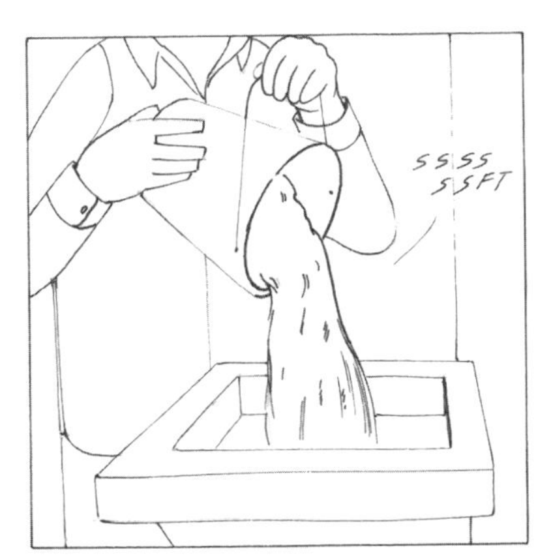
SSSS SSFT

TAP!
TAP!
TAP!

MONEY

JUST REGULAR PAPER

THESE PAPIER MACHÉ MASKS I MADE OF MY FATHER

ART HISTORICAL REFERENCES!
GOYA

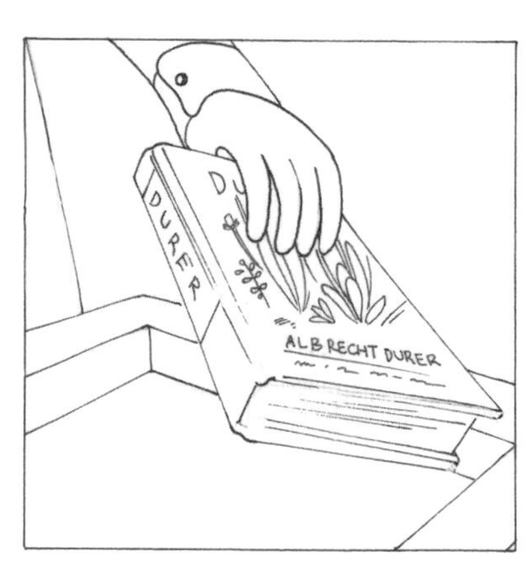
DURER
ALBRECHT DURER

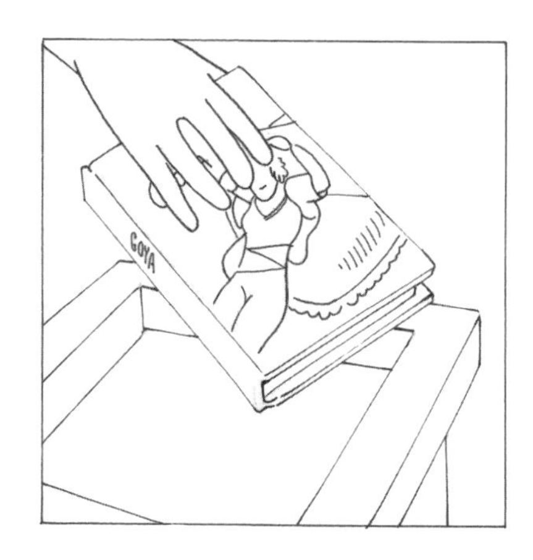
GOYA

THE SPINNING COGWHEELS I SEE SUPERIMPOSED OVER MY VISION DURING ANXIETY ATTACKS

REAL LIFE "OBSERVATIONS"

MEN ARE SOMETIMES
ORE ATTRACTIVE
HEN SEEN
M AFAR
THAN THEY ARE WHEN SEEN UP CLOSE

THE FINAL INGREDIENT NECESSARY FOR THE FUNCTIONING OF MY ART MAKING MACHINE ARE MY OWN HUMAN TEARS

EXCUSE ME A MOMENT

CAPITALISM
HOMOPHOBIA
INSTITUTIONALIZED RACISM
COLONIAL HISTORY
RAPE CULTURE
SYSTEMIC OPPRESSION

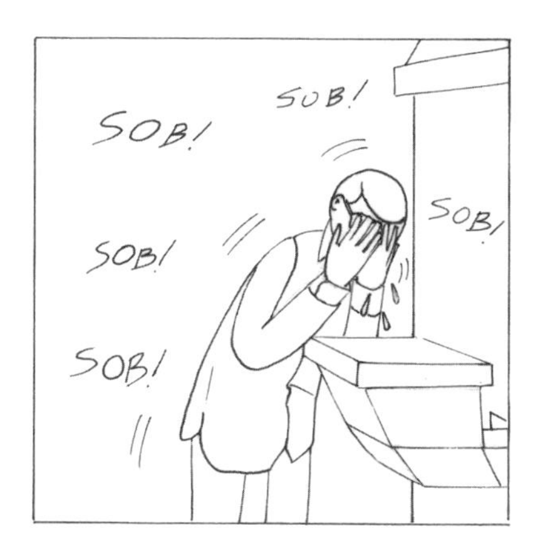
SOB!
SOB!
SOB!
SOB!
SOB!

RUMBLE!
RUMBLE!
RUMBLE!!
RUMBLE!
MYSTERY MACHINE

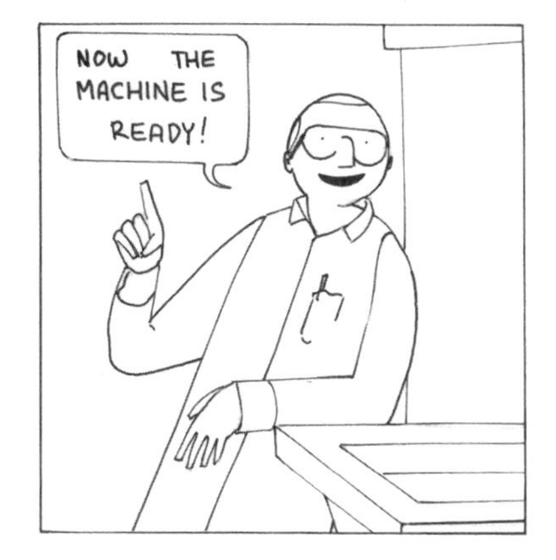
NOW THE MACHINE IS READY!

ONCE I PULL THIS LEVER...

... THE MACHINE BEGINS!

THE INGREDIENTS ARE PUT THROUGH A TOP SECRET "MATERIAL TRANSFORMATION"

RUMBLE -
RUMBLE
MYSTERY MACHINE

AND COME OUT THE OTHER END AS ART!

THE WHOLE PROCESS TAKES ABOUT AN HOUR

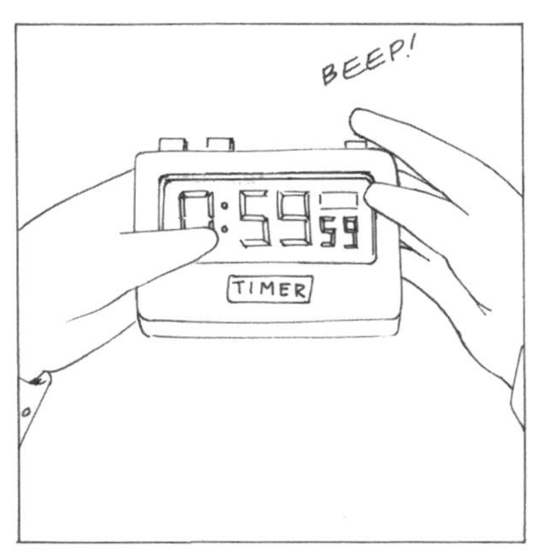
BEEP!
0:59
TIMER

EXCITING!

CAN I OFFER YOU A CUP OF COFFEE IN THE MEANTIME?

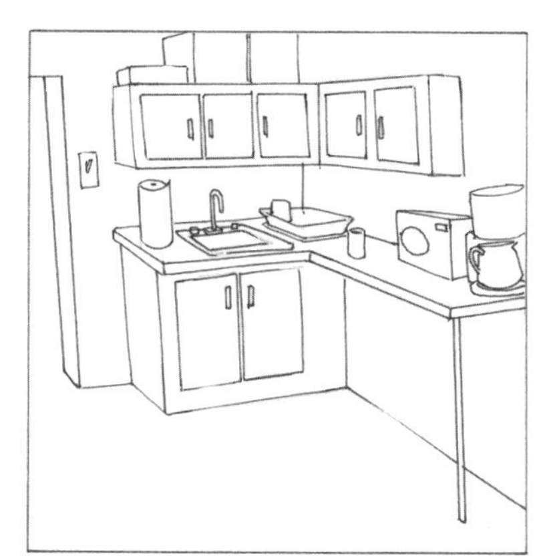

SSS
SSSS
SSSS

SO, HOW ARE YOU?

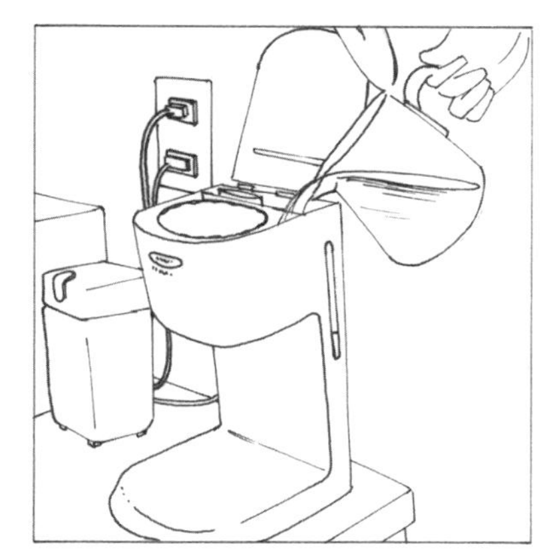

UH - HUH

PAT

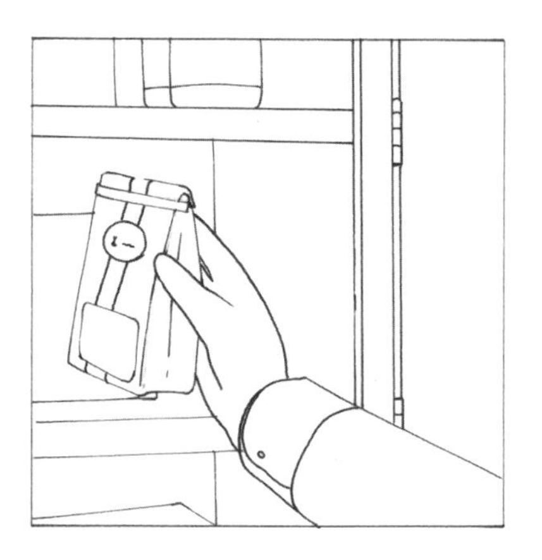

THAT'S NICE

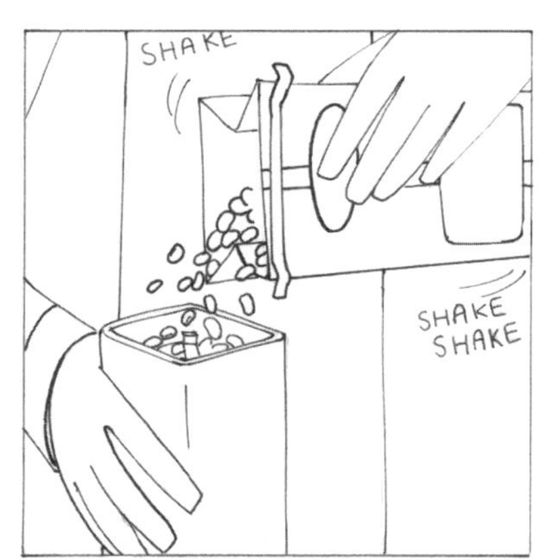
SHAKE
SHAKE SHAKE

BZZZZZZZZZZZZZZ
ZZZZZZ ZZZZZ
ZZZZZ Z Z ZZ
Z Z ZZZZ

OH
PAT
PAT PAT
HOW AM I?

CLICK!

. . .

I'M OKAY!

NO REALLY! I'M FINE!

HA HA!

. . .

BEEP BEEP!
BEEP BEEP!
BEEP BEEP!
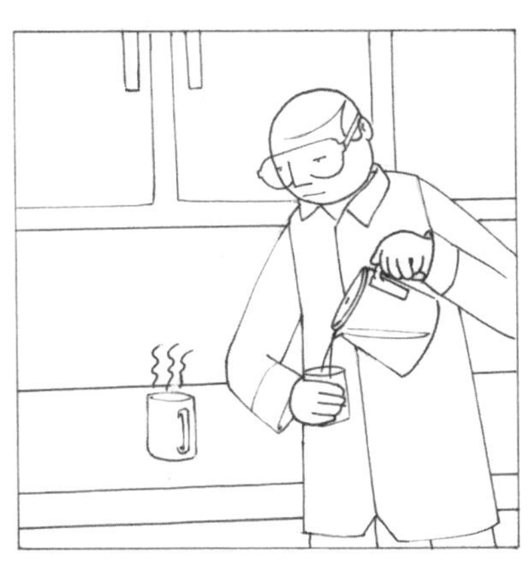

DO YOU EVER GET THE FEELING LIKE EVERYTHING YOU DO IS MEANINGLESS?

OH GOD! MY HEAD!
I'M SO TIRED!

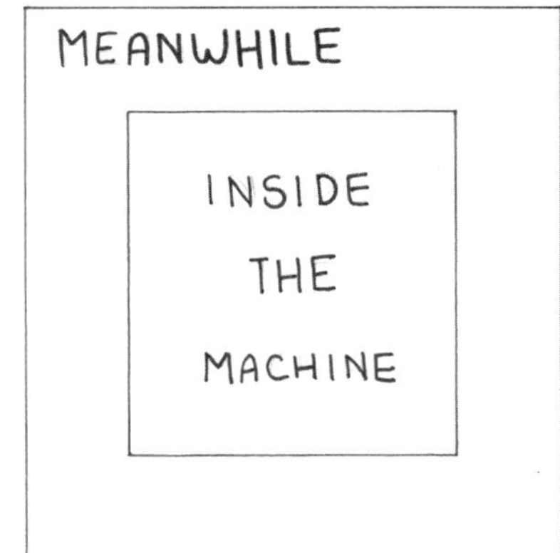
MEANWHILE
INSIDE THE MACHINE

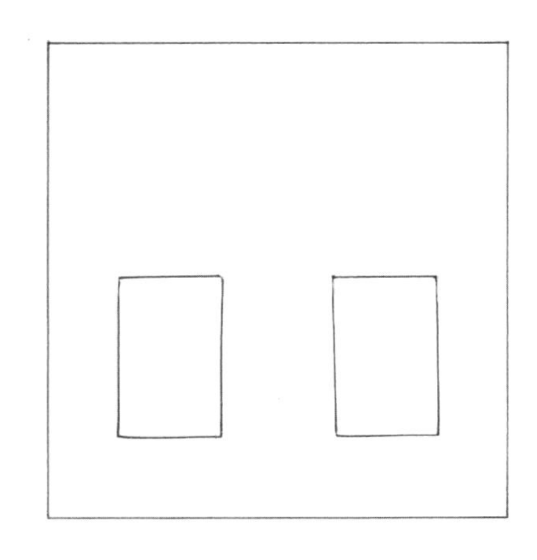

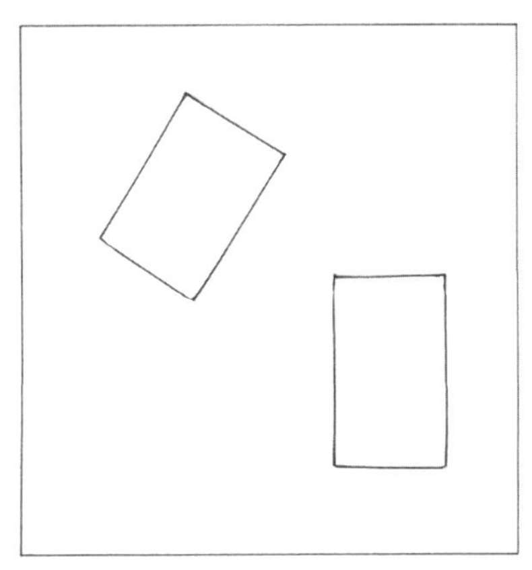

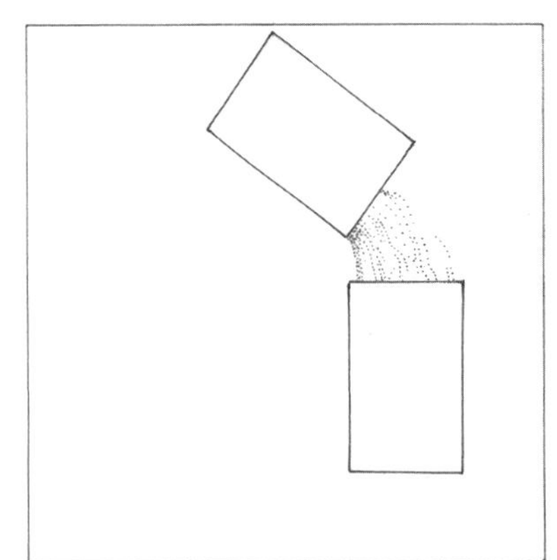

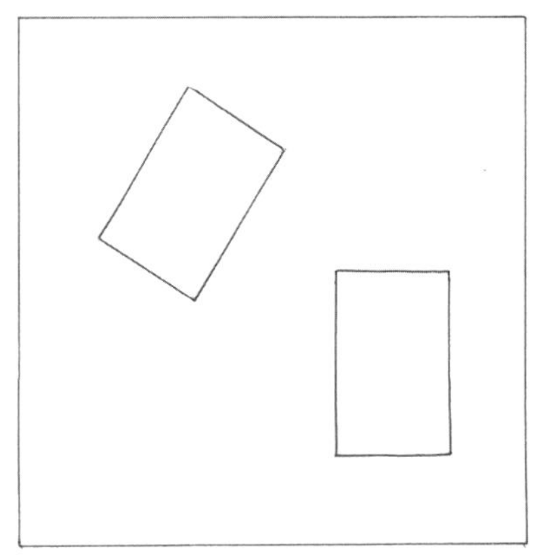

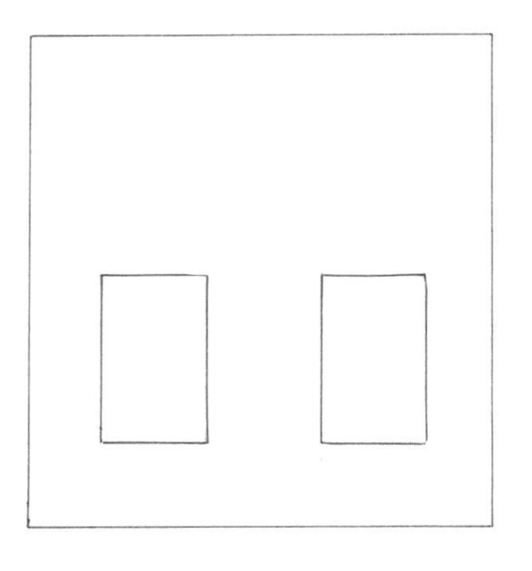

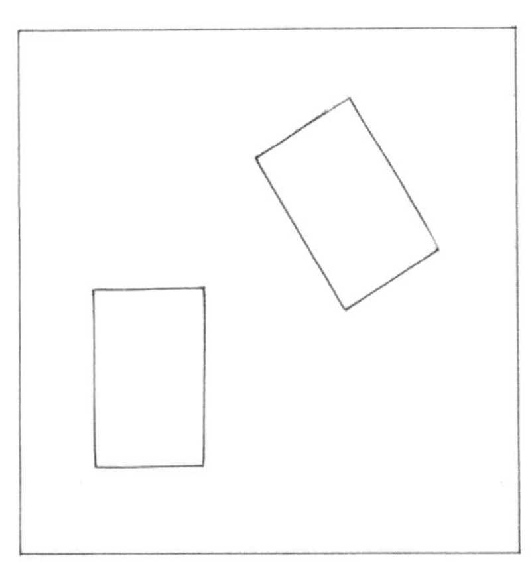

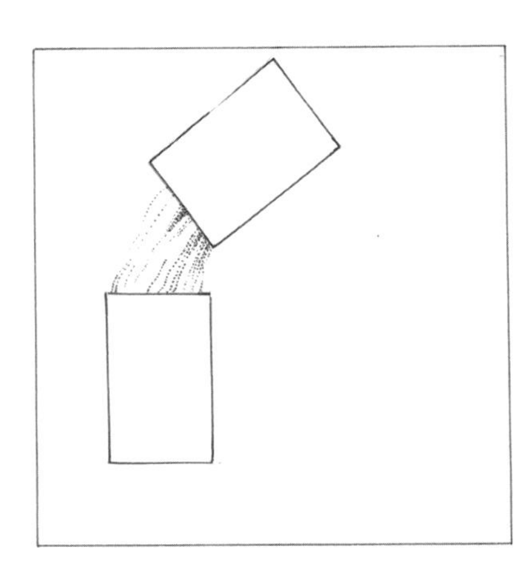

NO MATTER HOW HARD I TRY I JUST END UP FEELING ALIENATED FROM EVERY-ONE AROUND ME

UNABLE TO RELATE TO ANYONE

EVEN MY CLOSEST FRIENDS

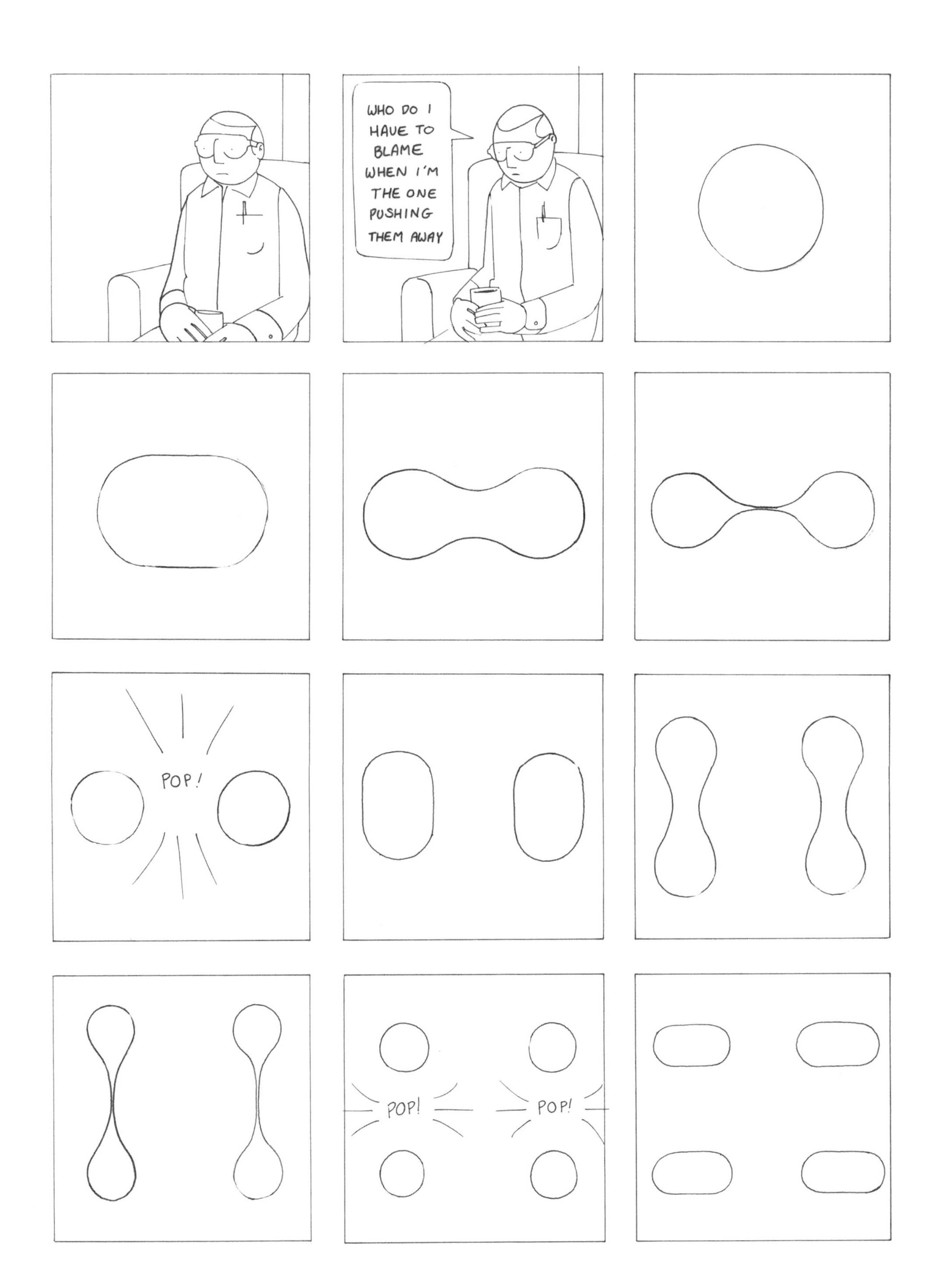
WHO DO I HAVE TO BLAME WHEN I'M THE ONE PUSHING THEM AWAY
POP!
POP!
POP!

I'M REALLY SMART

BUT I'M NOT HAPPY

I DON'T KNOW WHAT'S WRONG WITH ME

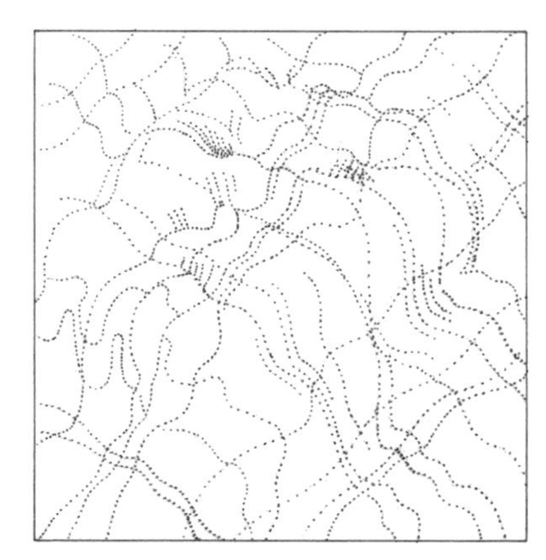

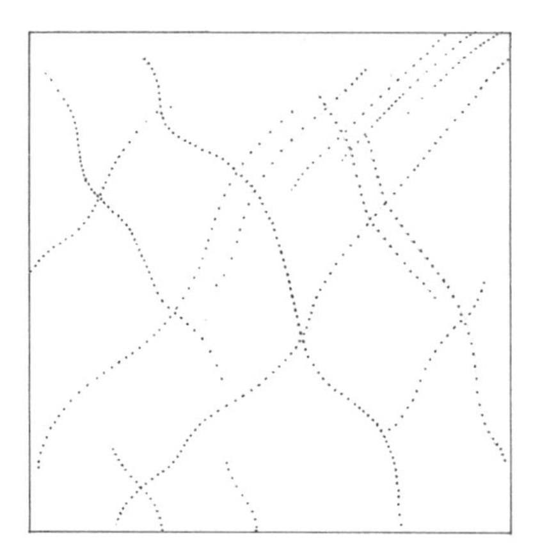

I'LL CUT THE TAB OF ACID IN HALF

AND TAKE HALF

AND THEN I MIGHT TAKE A WHOLE PILL OF ADDERALL

OR I MIGHT CUT THAT UP TOO AND JUST TAKE A LITTLE BIT

I'M NOT SUICIDAL

DON'T WORRY.

I JUST LIKE TO WRITE ABOUT SUICIDE

BECAUSE LIFE IS SO HORRIBLE

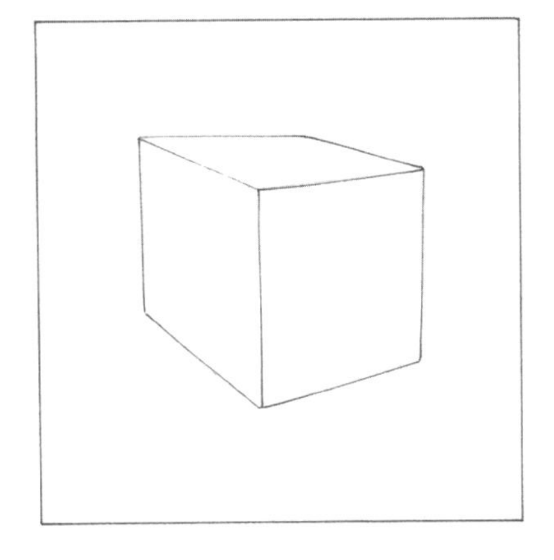

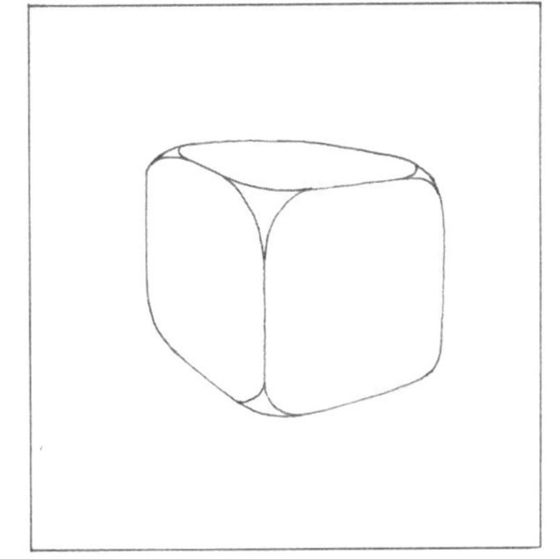

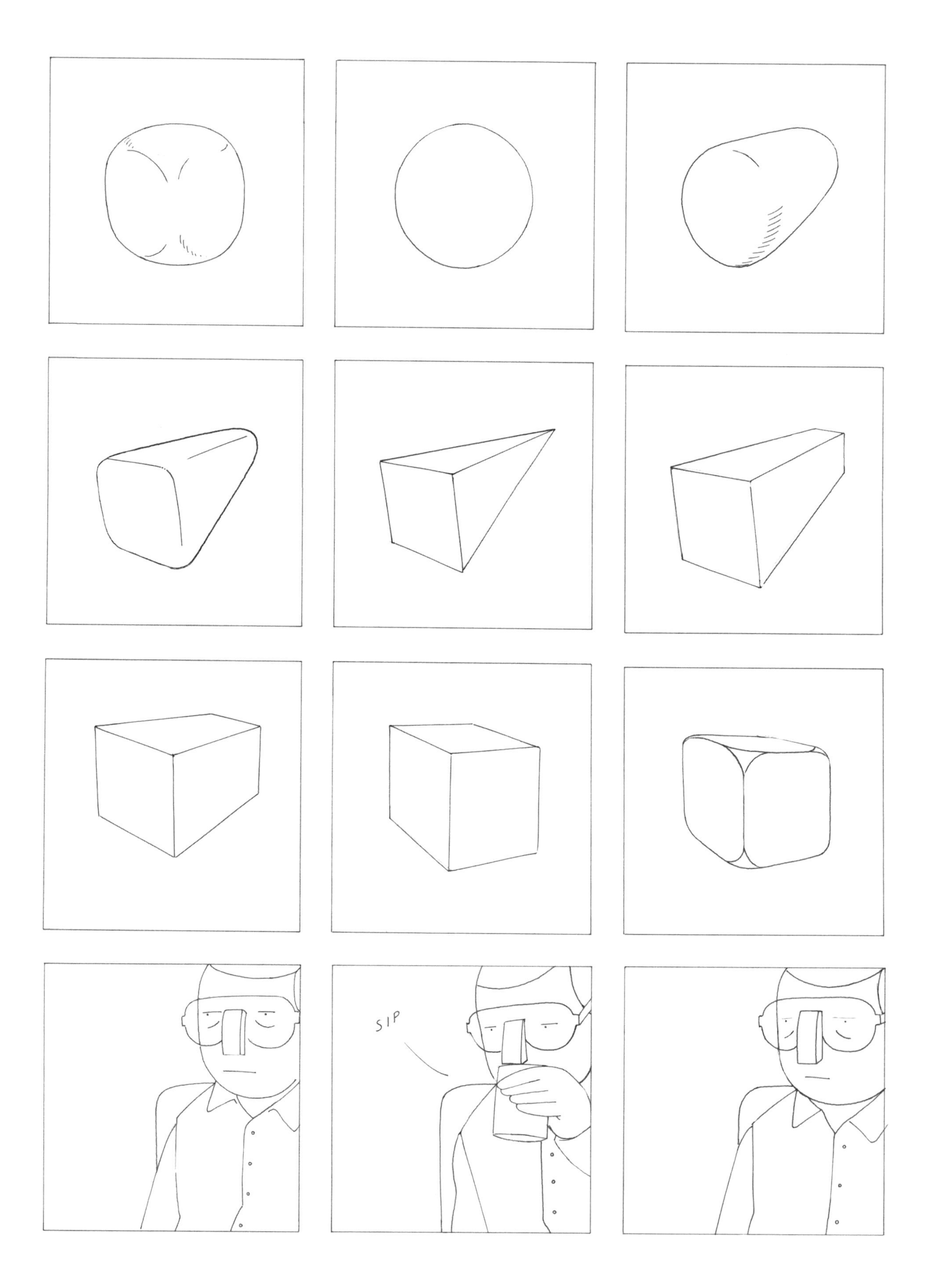
SIP

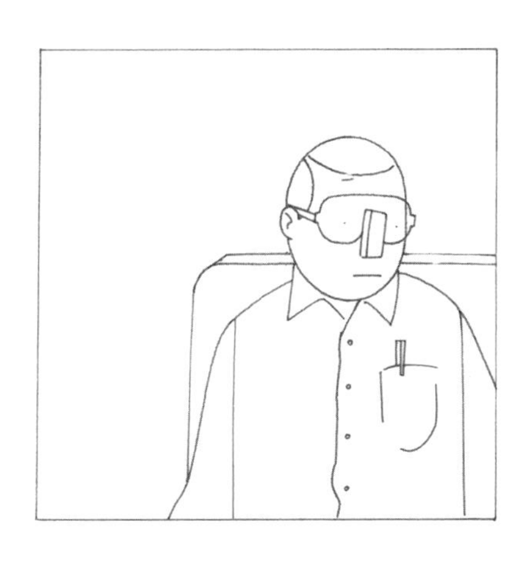
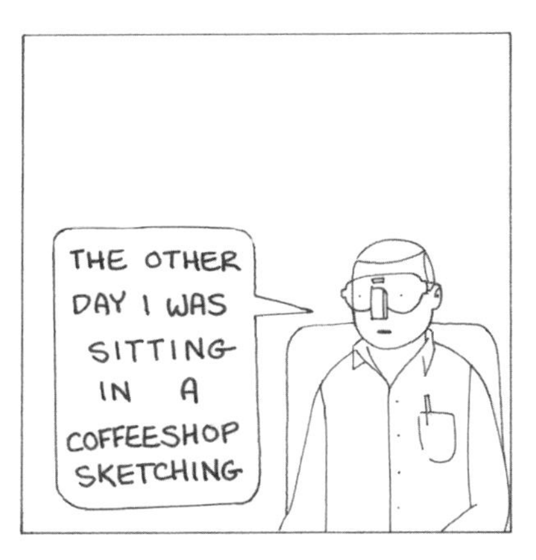
THE OTHER DAY I WAS SITTING IN A COFFEESHOP SKETCHING

AND I JUST STARTED THINKING ABOUT PEOPLE
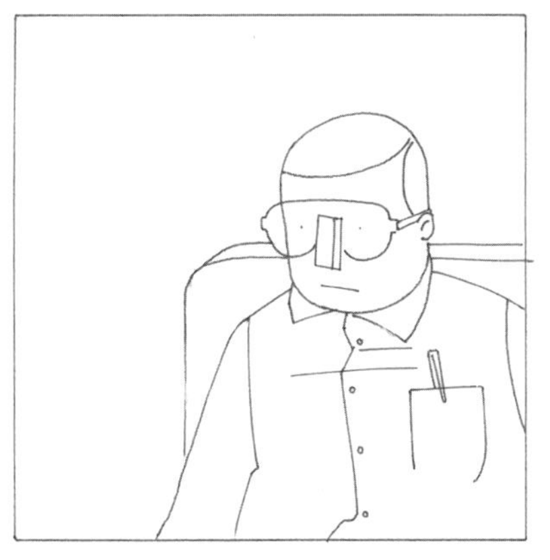

PSYCHOSIS

CAN MAYBE GRIP AN ENTIRE NATION

EVERYTHING IS TAINTED
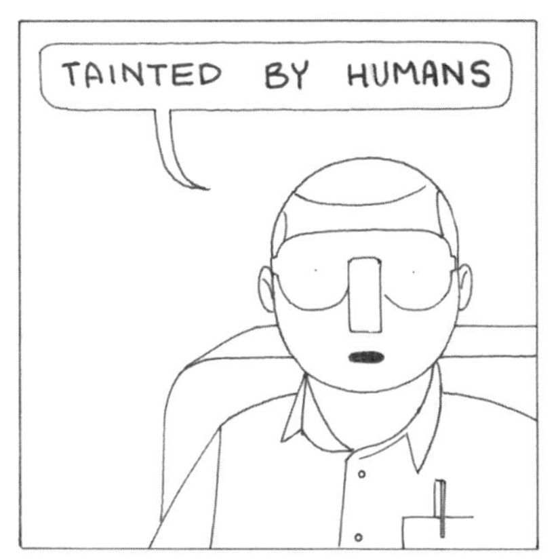
TAINTED BY HUMANS

AND I JUST STARTED CRYING

I WAS SO SCARED SOMEONE WOULD NOTICE ME CRYING AND THINK-

"WHY IS THAT MAN CRYING WHILE HE'S DRAWING ME?!"

SOMETIMES I JUST WANT TO SCREAM - YOU KNOW?!

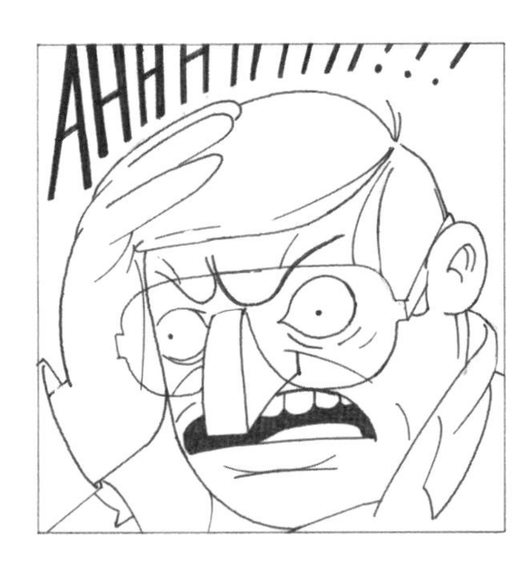
AHHHHHH!!!!

BWUHUHUHUUHUHH!
SOB!
SOB!
SOB!

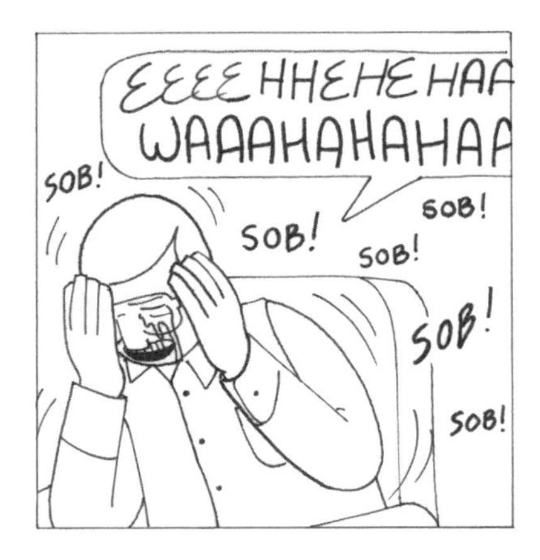
EEEEHHEHEHAA
WAAAHAHAHAA
SOB!
SOB!
SOB!
SOB!
SOB!
SOB!

BWUUHU
HUHUHU
UHU
I'M SORRY!!

YOU SHOULDN'T HAVE TO DEAL WITH THIS!!
SOB!
SOB!
SOB!

YOU JUST CAME TO SEE SOME STUPID ART!!

STUPID
STUPID!
STUPID!!

BEEP BEEP!
BEEP BEEP!
BEEP BEEP!
TIMER

BEEP BEEP!
BEE-
TIMER

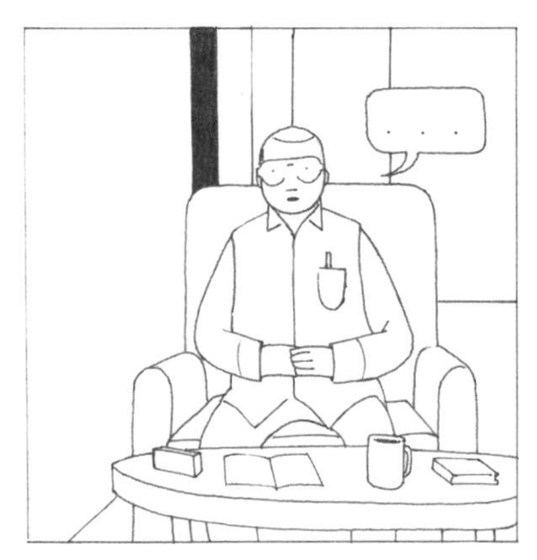
. . .

WELL, LET'S SEE HOW WE DID!

RUMBLE
RUMBLE
MYSTERY MACHINE

RUMBLE
RUMBLE
RUMBLE
ACHINE

PERFECT!

ANOTHER PERFECT ART OBJECT!

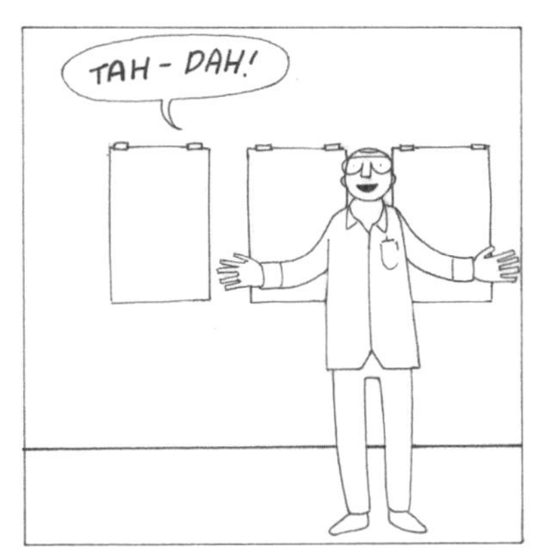
TAH-DAH!

THE HISTORY OF SEXUALITY

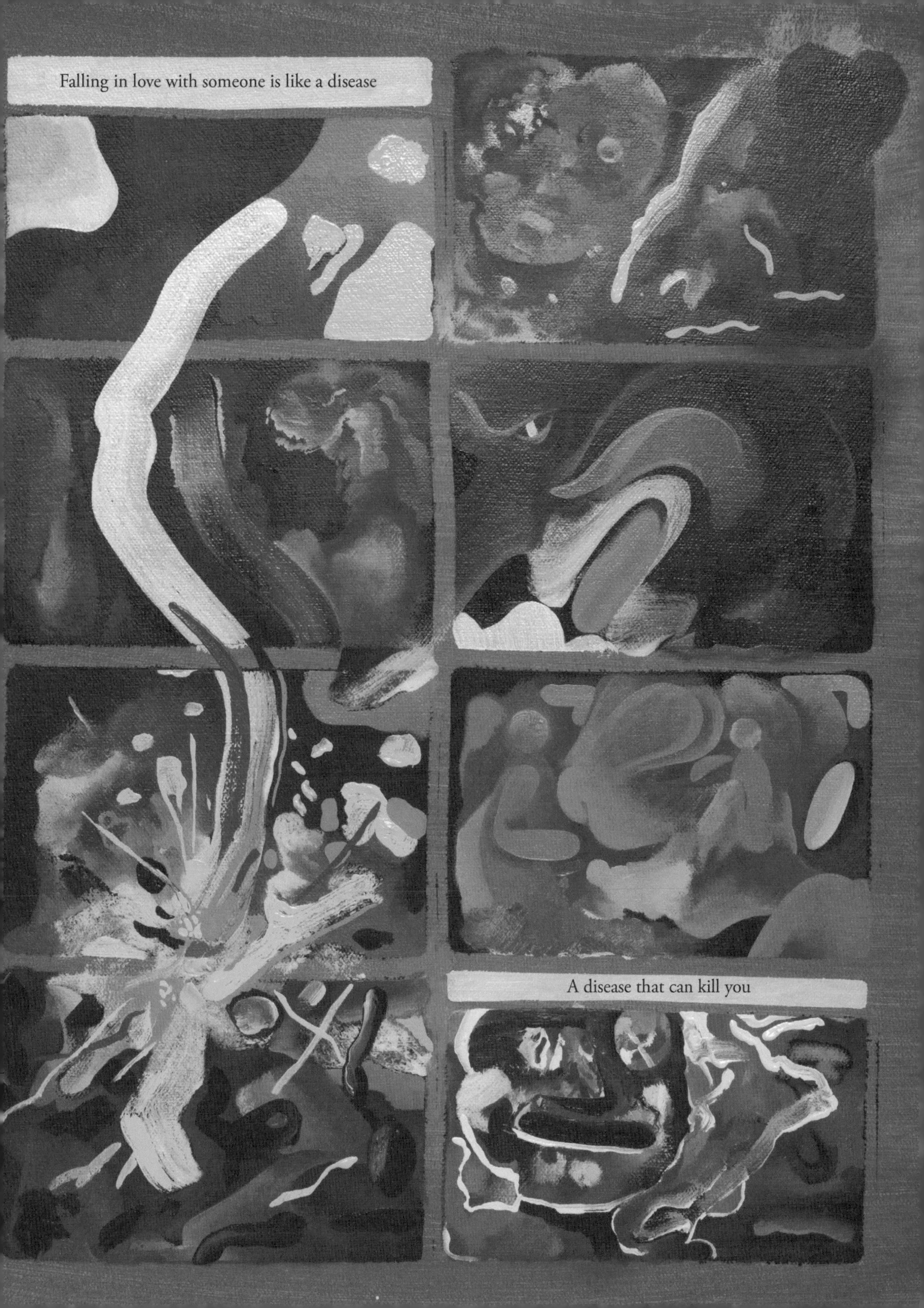
Falling in love with someone is like a disease
A disease that can kill you

Today I woke up at 4 a.m. to get to my job on the other side of town
I systematically arrange capital and merchandise for immediate consumption by drones
While I am gradually consumed by a disease that I don't understand

How can I explore my sexuality
within the vortex of fragmented identities
produced by false systems of representation

These are questions I avoid asking
myself instead basing my responses to external
stimuli purely on my immediate emotional reaction

I sleep with a new man every night

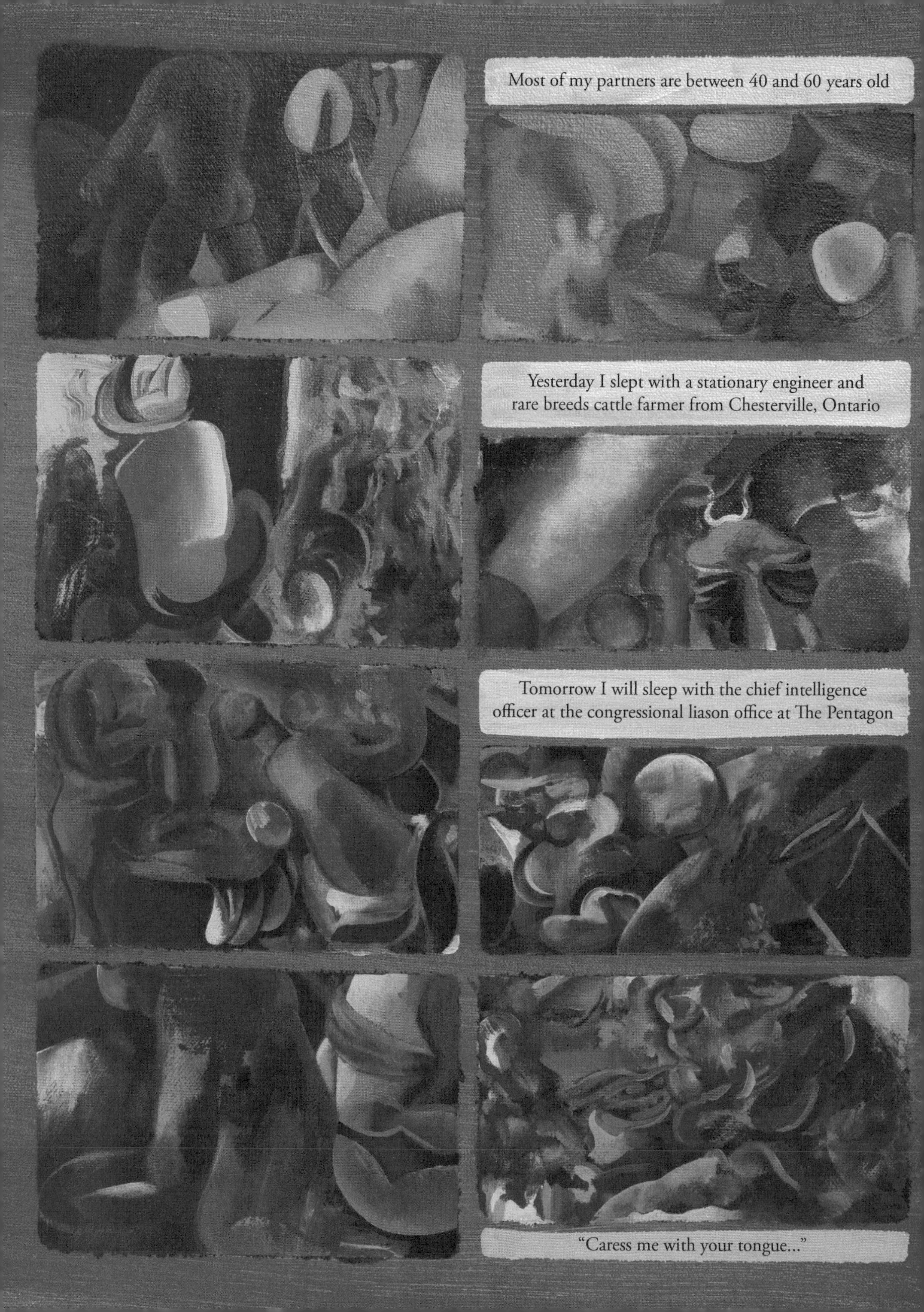
Most of my partners are between 40 and 60 years old
Yesterday I slept with a stationary engineer and
rare breeds cattle farmer from Chesterville, Ontario
Tomorrow I will sleep with the chief intelligence
officer at the congressional liason office at The Pentagon
“Caress me with your tongue...”

Multiple orders of self-referential simulations
reverse the understood definition of beauty

Beauty is now poison

Who am I if I don't know how to love

Ways of Seeing

The Performative ally

I NEED TO GET MY HAIRCUT JUST RIGHT FOR THIS POLITICAL PROTEST!

I NEED TO FIND JUST THE RIGHT SECOND HAND T-SHIRT!
MENS

I AM - A "PERFORMATIVE ALLY"...

FREE PALEST~~E~~INE!!
ND
PATION
SNAP!
I GO WHERE I AM NEEDED...

GAY CLUBS...

. . . A SAFE SPACE TO PICK UP GIRLS!

MY LIBERAL ARTS PROGRAM TEACHES ME ABOUT THE DEVELOPING WORLD

THANKS MOM AND DAD!!
MUJI

The Gatekeeper

MY MOTHER IS A BLACK LATINA LESBIAN - MY FATHER AN EMPOVERISHED SCHIZOPHRENIC MUSLIM

I AM A NONBINARY SOCIALIST REVOLUTIONARY WITH NARCOLEPSY - THEY CALL ME . . .
"THE GATE KEEPER"

I LIVE OFF SPROUTED GRAINS I'VE PROCURED THROUGH A COMMUNITY BASED BARTERING SYSTEM

FOR THESE BARE NECESSITIES I TRADE MY SERVICES AS A BICYCLE REPAIR PERSON, OR ELSE THE MAGIC MUSHROOMS I GROW IN THE CORNER OF MY SHANTY

I HAVE A REVERSE CARBON FOOTPRINT OF -600 ppm...
...I'VE NEVER ATTENDED ANY TYPE OF SCHOOL ...

... AND I'VE ASSASSINATED 3 OF THE WORLD'S TOP NEOLIBERAL ECONOMISTS

White Passing

I TALK JUST LIKE THEM...
MY SKIN LOOKS JUST LIKE THEIRS...

BUT NONE OF THEM KNOW MY SECRET...
I AM ...
"WHITE PASSING"...

MORE MAYONNAISE FOR YOUR KALE CHIPS SAMUEL?
UHH...
?!
-YEAH!

PERFECT COTTAGE WEATHER WE'RE HAVING
WHERE IS YOUR FAMILY'S SUMMER HOME, SAMUEL?

...
IT'S IN
UHH...
WEST-MORE
...
ING-
TON
ANOTHER CRISIS AVERTED, YET I MUST REMAIN VIGILANT

LIKE THE SWORD OF DAMOCLES HANGING ABOVE MY HEAD ANY MOMENT MY WHITE PRIVILEGE CAN BE REVOKED
JOB FAIR
CV
WHAT A CUTE WAY TO SPELL SAMMY!

Ashamed

WEALTHY, PRIVILEGED, I HAVE EVERYTHING I COULD EVER WANT
AND YET... THIS PERSISTENT FEELING

I AM...
"ASHAMED"

EVERYWHERE I GO THEY SCREAM SHAME AT ME

WHEN I FLIRT WITH WHITE SUPREMACY THEY SAY SHAME TO ME

WHEN I DISMANTLE THEIR UNIONS THEY SAY SHAME TO ME AGAIN

MY CRUSHING SHAME...
EVER-PRESENT UNBEARABLE

Amidst the wreckage of climate apocalypse an enclave of lgbtq warriors has carved out a nation state in what is left of the barren wasteland formerly known as California

Queernofornia is a perfect utopia.

You are now a citizen, welcome.

Each new citizen undergoes a mandatory screening in which they are assigned a score along the intersectionality index

REMEMBER TO BE AS DETAILED AS POSSIBLE WHEN COMPLETING THE SECTION ON YOUR ANCESTRAL HERITAGE

Based on their assessment citizens are awarded reparations relative to the level of discrimination they were faced with in the old world
$50000
FIFTY THOUSAND
GAY DOLLARS

The people of Queernofornia harvest energy from sucking dick & eating pussy & ass in tantric orgone accumulation sex practices which they use to power their cities

This libidinal energy has rejuvenated Queernofornia's natural environment

Flowers bloom, rivers & streams spring up terraforming an otherwise lethal & uninhabitable expanse of desert

Hordes of straight climate refugees continuously assault the gates of Queernafornia frequently erupting into armed conflict

Allies are granted asylum, but segregated to an artificial off-shore island and closely monitored

HELLO, MY NAME IS SUNNY. I AM WRITING A STORY ABOUT MIGRATION & DIASPORA & INTERVIEWING NEW CITIZENS. CAN I ASK YOU SOME QUESTIONS?

OKAY, GREAT!
LET'S BEGIN

HOW IS NATIONAL IDENTITY CONSTRUCTED?

WHO HAS THE POWER TO CREATE BORDERS AND TO ARCHIVE HISTORY?

IF WE WERE CAPABLE OF FEELING THE PAIN OF OTHERS WOULD WE EVER BE ABLE TO FEEL ANY-THING OTHER THAN PAIN?

THANK YOU FOR YOUR TIME, THESE ARE ALL VALUABLE INSIGHTS & I'LL BE SURE TO LIST YOU AMONG THE DEDICATIONS WHEN MY NOVEL IS PUBLISHED.

Afterwards, Sunny goes down on you

A few weeks later Sunny disappears, you know not to ask questions & quickly forget that he ever existed
ROOM FOR RENT
FREE
FREE

A few decades pass, you've now lived in Queernofornia longer than you've lived anywhere else. How much of you is from where?

Do you feel like this land belongs to you? Where is your family? All you have is yourself. You fall in love with someone who looks just like Sunny Balwani

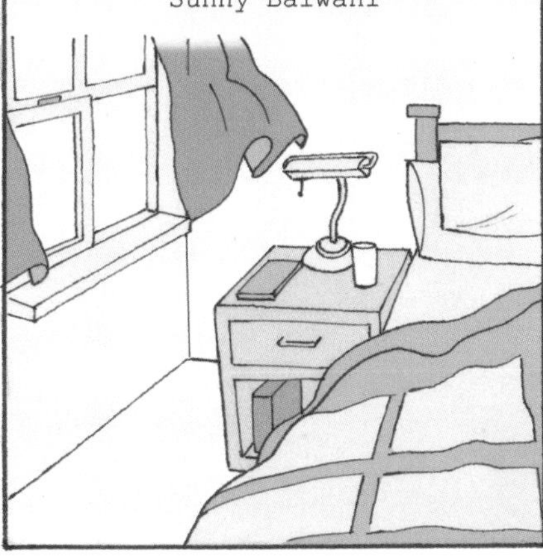

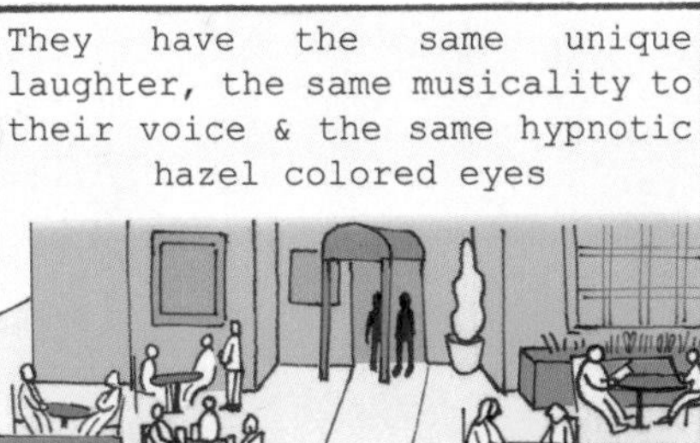

They have the same unique laughter, the same musicality to their voice & the same hypnotic hazel colored eyes

On your anniversary, sitting in a crowded restaurant, they hand you a book

I FOUND YOUR NAME LISTED AMONG THE DEDICATIONS. ARE YOU FAMILIAR WITH THE AUTHOR?

I RECOGNIZE THIS PROSE STYLE AS THAT OF AN OLD FRIEND BUT THE NAME IS CHANGED

I COULDN'T FIND ANY INFORMATION ON HIM. IT'S LIKE HE DOESN'T EXIST.
NEW STORIES
SAMI ALWANI

THANK YOU FOR THIS
I LOVE YOU HABIBI

You share a kiss, your spouse's tongue slips into your mouth

A bomb explodes collapsing the main entrance

You and your partner try to escape through a side door but straight liberation forces are waiting outside and gun you both down

Simmie Antflick is a man reduced to emptiness, the soot and ash which are the remnants of their stinging degradation fill them, leaving no room for anything else.

They have been stewing in bitterness for years, drinking from an overflowing cup of bitterness perhaps their whole life or at least as far back as those cacophonous memories of violence can be traced, those memories which echo, soundless and mournful, across generations, so that it might be said that Simmie had been nursed on bitterness for many centuries before he was even born.

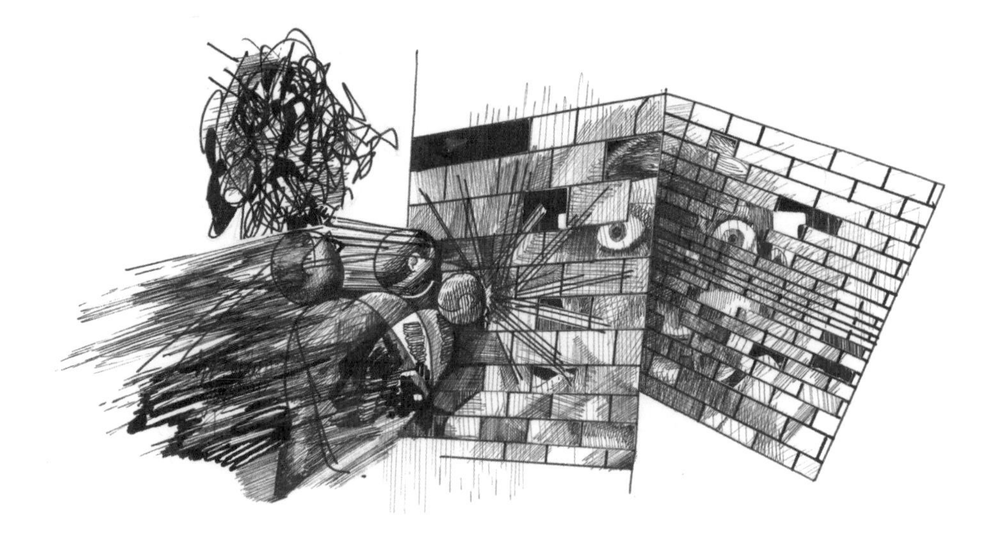

Simmie can't stop thinking about white supremac

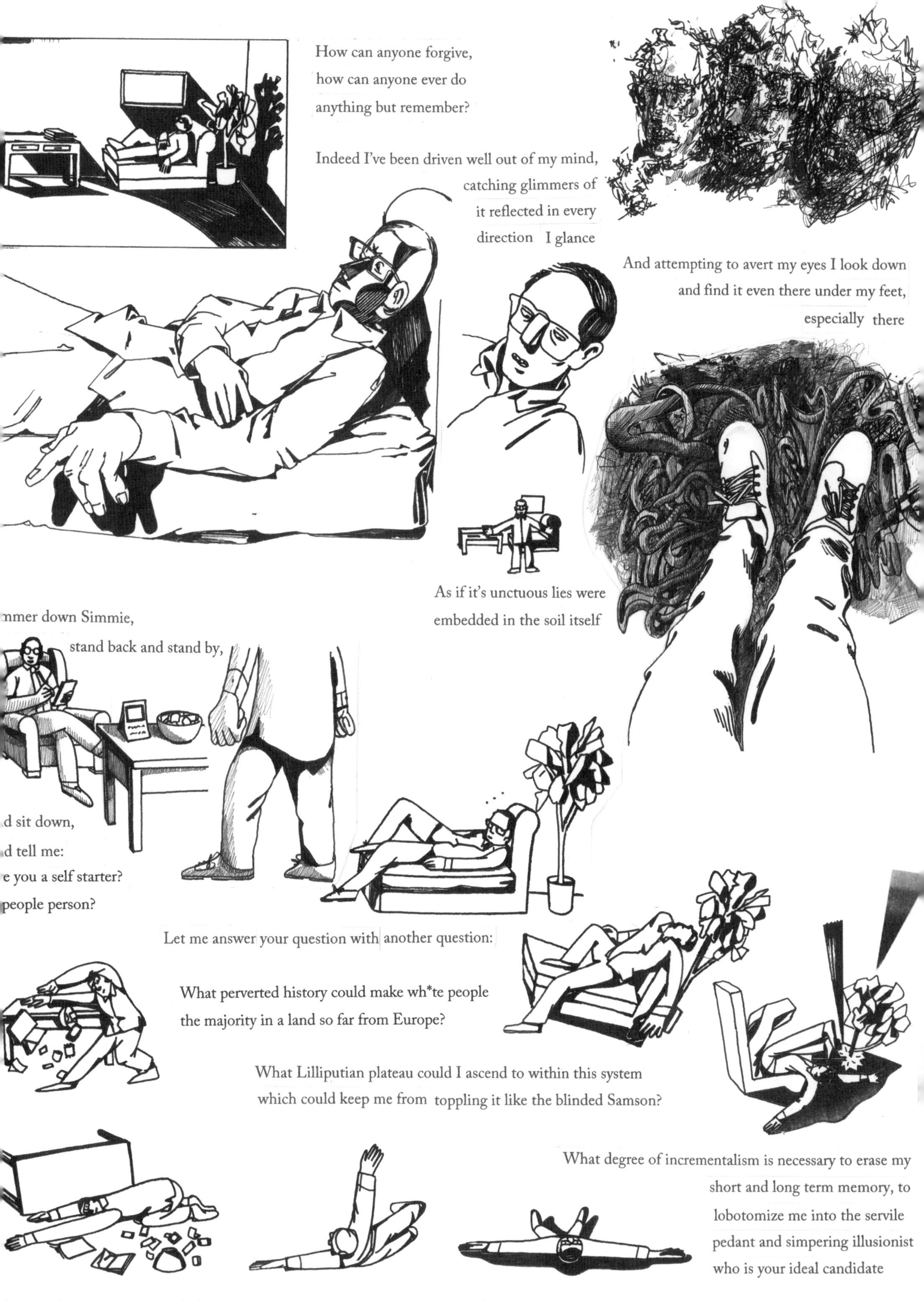

How can anyone forgive,
how can anyone ever do
anything but remember?
Indeed I've been driven well out of my mind,
catching glimmers of
it reflected in every
direction I glance
And attempting to avert my eyes I look down
and find it even there under my feet,
especially there
As if it's unctuous lies were
embedded in the soil itself
mmer down Simmie,
stand back and stand by,
d sit down,
d tell me:
e you a self starter?
people person?
Let me answer your question with another question:
What perverted history could make wh*te people
the majority in a land so far from Europe?
What Lilliputian plateau could I ascend to within this system
which could keep me from toppling it like the blinded Samson?
What degree of incrementalism is necessary to erase my
short and long term memory, to
lobotomize me into the servile
pedant and simpering illusionist
who is your ideal candidate

My resentment is an armor, it protects me, my dreams for the future pulverized into shining scales I adorn myself with
The glittering of your scales sure is scintillating and hypnotic Simmie who woulda thought they were born from such unbearable suffering
It is the very virtue of bearing the unbearable which imbues them with such intoxicating beauty
Each sliver: carmine, sapphire, chartreuse, chromatic aberrations of blinding intensity
A pressure worse than that required to explode an atom bomb can produce diamonds
In fact I kinda find them sorta sensual… wouldn't it be nice to commune over our shared traumas?

Quit equivocating, I wanna touch you Simmie, but these scales are sewn into your skin, what's beneath?
However useful, trauma is a strong word that has come to define perhaps too broad a range of experiences
Simmie can scarcely hide the tremors in his breath, his awareness of his own body amplifies, and then subdivides infinitely as he explains away his own identity as easily as if it were a fractal equation
(Is their queerness simply a mask disguising the positionality of their privilege?)
The only thing in me stronger than my resentment: my libido
"Stick your thing in me Simmie!"

"Civilization"
Cowards! Your greatest failure is a lack of imagination
To forsake a perfect world and
instead spend decades scaffolding
the dreams of psychopaths
Swallowing bleached-white bones
alongside banal luxuries by the fistful
CANNABIS
ON
DUTY PAID
CANADA
DROIT ACQUITTÉ
CANNABIS
ON
DUTY PAID
CANADA
DROIT ACQUITTÉ
Thinking this system will spare you the same
violence it administers
to those it others
The treasure they tease you with crumbles as soon as you hold it in your han

The Law"
ITEMS INCLUDED IN THE SHIPMENT
QTY ITEM NAME
1 NO LONGER HUMAN
The delicacies
upon which you feast
still leave you hungry
You eat,
swallowing
complacency,
swallowing time,
like Saturn
devouring
his son
onsuming endlessly, like a conflagration devouring a vast wilderness
nd are never sated
Until upon your passing, put out to pasture, your swollen distended
belly erupts like a nest of spiders
Releasing those parasites
you've lovingly incubated
And looking down at your
own venerable corpse you find
In feasting you had been feasted upon

Simmie - the unique character of your misery is hysterical to me
Normally I just shoo away demands for accountability like so many fr
flies circling my gooseberry fool
But for some reason your impot
indictments of the status quo lea
me trembling with laughter
Racked by paroxysms of debilitating laughter
An exotic blend of complex trauma, psychotic ramblings and spicy gay high aesthetic make you a hit at the dinner party while remaining just pathetic enough to be non-threatening
Varsity
Aud #8
Row: H Seat: 9
CINEPLE
70MM JOKER
[CC]
Sun 07:20p 13/10/19
Perhaps your special brand of mental illness is marketable?
Have you tried Stand Up?
'Tis I, Antflick, your favorite 30 year old baby and hideous bouffant
It has been said that laughter is the best medicine so I have prepared a regimen of "Impressions" to treat your affliction:
"Modernity," (for which there is no cur
before it metastasizes and overtakes yo

"SIMPLE SIMON"

An Academic:

"Look at me,
I'm an academic:
Nothing is absolute!
Different things are
true at different
times!"

"Oh no! I spilled latte on my Kobo!
Now how will I finish reading
my Michael Parenti eBook?!"

Gentry:

"A tennis ball can be a mandala"

"With the acquisition of
these knock-off Renoirs my Victorian-style
home's aestheticization of a historical golden
era of class power is complete, and I can now
host my Downton Abbey watch-parties in peace"

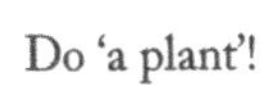
Do 'a plant'!

A plant:

"Now I am a plant! I photosynthesize!"

"I choke and die!"
cough cough cough
"Immolation…"
fall

"Humans are
so dumb…"

**How Dumb
Are They?!**

"Humans are
so dumb: they
are the stupidest
fucking animal
that has ever
existed. God
created us and
then laughed
and then wept
and then left"

GEN1 SEC./SEC. GA0 ROW/RANGÉE 21 SEAT/SIÈGE ANE 0.00 PRICE TYPE/PRIX TYPE

$ $0.00 CONVENIENCE CHARGE

GEN1 SEC./SEC.

Taxi Driver

TIFF Bell Lightbox, Cinema 4

ROW/RANGÉE SEAT/SIÈGE
GA0 21

Sunday December 01, 2019 7:15 PM

11/24/2019

It's funny how ideas form, slowly
It's like a process of erosion, reality is a cliff-face
which the ocean of your thoughts
and actions lash at continuously
Until the stone
has been softened,
and dissolves into
sediment
Reality is a racist, repulsive
and murderous formation of earth,
which we take as foundational
You have an idea to bake a pie
You begin to list and visualize each ingredient and compare
the list to the contents of your pantry and refrigerator
And those ingredients you don't have on hand you make plans to procure
Each task is divided into a series
of subtasks, creating a network,
Which you integrate into the
larger list of tasks you plan to
accomplish that day, or in the
following days
And the process of dissolving that earth is a historical process

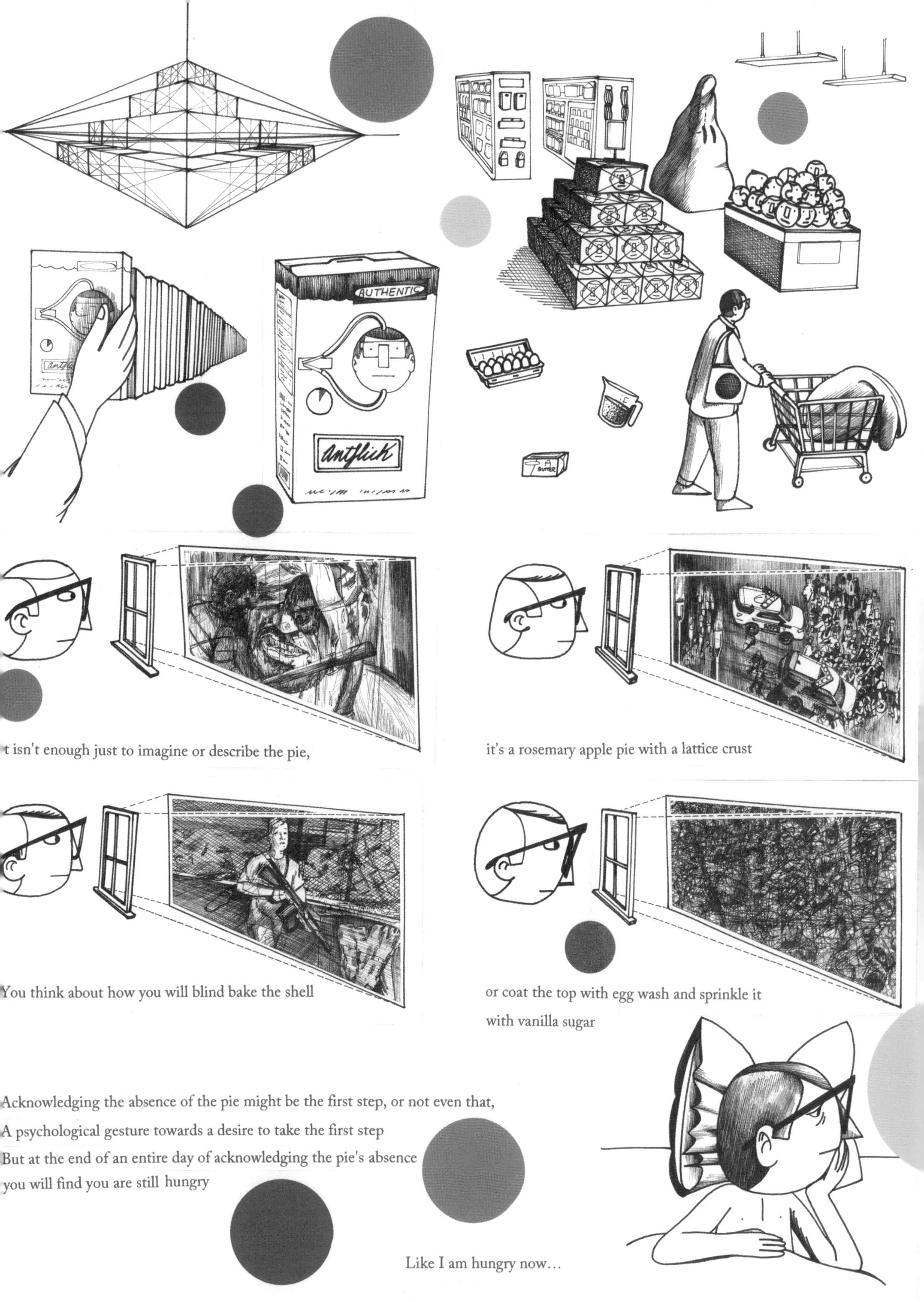
AUTHENTIC
antflick
t isn't enough just to imagine or describe the pie,
it's a rosemary apple pie with a lattice crust
You think about how you will blind bake the shell
or coat the top with egg wash and sprinkle it
with vanilla sugar
Acknowledging the absence of the pie might be the first step, or not even that,
A psychological gesture towards a desire to take the first step
But at the end of an entire day of acknowledging the pie's absence
you will find you are still hungry
Like I am hungry now...

THE DEAD
FATHER

THE
DEAD
FATHER

IT'S A BOY!
WAHHH!!
WAAHHHH!

NOW SON, YOU'VE GOT A FEW OPTIONS

YOU CAN BECOME AN ACTOR OR A MUSICIAN OR A DANCER- OR A WRITER OR ARTIST OR CARTOONIST ... LIKE ME

OR YOU COULD BE A DOCTOR OR A LAWYER OR A PROFESSOR OR A DIRECTOR OR A MATH-EMATICIAN OR A PEDIATRICIAN OR A SCIENTIST, PHYSICIST OR ENGINEER... LIKE MY FATHER

OR ELSE ANY OTHER OF AN UNENDING AND LIMITLESS LIST OF POSSIBLE FUTURE OCCUPATIONS INCLUDING BUT NOT LIMITED TO:
• PHYSICAL THERAPIST
• ACCOUNTANT
• CARPEN
• COMPUTER TECHNICIAN
• YOJIMBO
REAL ESTATE AGENT
• INVESTMENT BANKER
LLGIRL
OR ORNITHOL
OR OPTHAMO
OR GYNACOLOG

BUT WHATEVER YOU DO CHOOSE JUST BE SURE THAT ALL YOUR ACTIONS ARE GUIDED BY AN INESCAPABLE UNDER-STANDING THAT YOU AS A PERSON ARE FUNDAMENTALLY INSUFFICIENT AND THAT YOUR CAPACITY TO WORK IS THE ONLY CAPACITY IN WHICH YOU ARE VALUABLE

• • •

AN ELECTRIC TENSION FLITS FROM HEAD TO HEAD IN THE PRESS ROOM
TAP TAP TAP TAP TAP TAP TAP TAP TAP TAP TAP TAP TAP TAP TAP TAP TAP
THE ENDS OF DOZENS OF CARBON PENCILS ANXIOUSLY TAPPING DOZENS OF WIREBOUND REPORTER'S NOTEBOOKS COMPOSE A MINIATURE ORCHESTRA OF ANTICIPATORY DRUMROLL AS THE COLLECTED PRESS AWAITS THEIR FIRST CONFERENCE WITH THE FIRST-BORN SON OF AMERICA'S GREATEST LIVING HERO- SAMI ALWANI

A HUSH FALLS OVER THE ROOM AS THE SQUEAKING OF CARRIAGE WHEELS ANNOUNCES THE BABY'S ARRIVAL...

THANK YOU FOR COMING LADIES AND GENTLEMEN

WE ARE PLEASED TO HAVE YOU ALL HERE TO ANNOUNCE THE BIRTH AND SUCCESSFUL DELIVERY OF MY CHILD- BABY ALWANI. I WILL KEEP THIS INTRO-DUCTION SHORT AS I KNOW THERE IS A LOT TO DISCUSS, SUFFICE TO SAY, BABY WILL BE HAPPY TO ANSWER ALL OF YOUR QUESTIONS

BABY! BABY!
BABY, DO YOU KNOW WHERE YOU ARE?!
HOW DO YOU FEEL?! HOW ARE YOU FEELING??!!
WHAT DO YOU LIKE TO DO WITH YOUR DAYS OFF BABY?!

BABY! WHO WILL YOU MARRY?!
WHAT IS YOUR FAVORITE COLOR?!
HOW CAN WE KNOW WHAT IS RIGHT?!
BABY! BABY! WHY SHOULD WE BE INTERESTED IN WHAT YOU HAVE TO SAY?!

-WARHOL
-BERGMAN'S PERSONA

I HAVE...
A PAUSE

I HAVE A SPECIAL KIND OF UNDERSTANDING OF MAN...
AN UNDERSTANDING THAT RENDERS CERTAIN ASPECTS OF REALITY ACCESSIBLE TO ME THAT OTHERS MIGHT NOT SEE...

IT ISN'T THAT MEN HIDE THESE THINGS FROM THEMSELVES BUT PERHAPS THEY HAVE NO TIME OR DO NOT CARE TO SEE THEM.

THERE IS ANOTHER REALITY IN MEN PROJECTED ALONGSIDE WHAT IS OBVIOUS ABOUT THEM
A REALITY MADE UP OF THOUSANDS OF ELEGANTLY DESCRIBED ARCS AND GESTURES - WORDS, MOUTHED IN A SECRET LANGUAGE OF FLESH, TALKING ALL THE TIME

TALKING IN YOUR EYES, SPREAD ACROSS YOUR LIPS- INVISIBLE THOUGHTS ESCAPING IN THE ARTICULATION AND ARRANGE-MENT OF YOUR LIMBS

A RESIDUAL ACCUMULATION OF EXPERIENCES COMPOSES YOUR IDENTITY IN THE SAME WAY A FACE IS PAINTED IN COUNTLESS MINUTE AND TRANSPARENT GLAZES
OF COURSE, IT ISN'T NECESSARY TO SEE EVERY BRUSH STROKE TO ENJOY THE PICTURE

... BUT YOU SEE...?

... WELL...

THEN WHAT IS IT THAT YOU SEE?

• • •

BABY KNOCKS ON HIS FATHER'S BEDROOM DOOR TO ASK HIM A QUESTION AND PUSHES THE DOOR OPEN WHEN HE HEARS NO RESPONSE

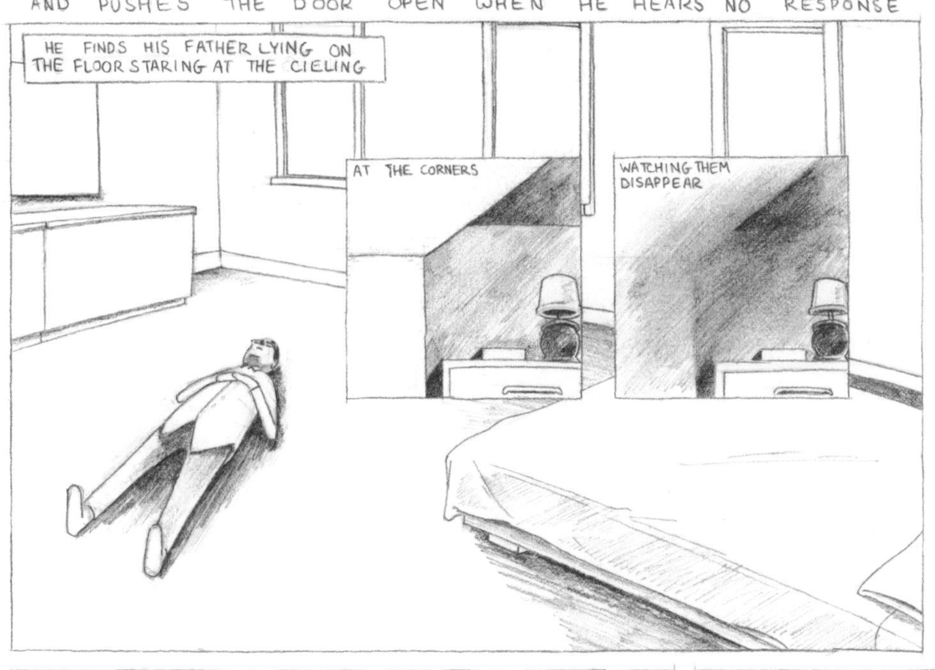
HE FINDS HIS FATHER LYING ON THE FLOOR STARING AT THE CIELING
AT THE CORNERS
WATCHING THEM DISAPPEAR

BABY FORGETS HIS QUESTION AND SITS DOWN BESIDE HIS FATHER
WHAT ARE YOU THINKING ABOUT?

NOTHING
BUT REALLY SAMI HAD BEEN THINKING ABOUT HIS PICTURES

THE OTHER DAY HE PAINTED A VIOLENT PICTURE OF HIM-SELF AS A ZOMBIE, AND HE HAD BEEN THINKING
"IS THAT HOW I REALLY FEEL?"
AND THEN:
"YES, I GUESS IT MUST BE"

SAMI'S ATTENTION SHIFTS TO A PATCH OF LIGHT ON THE WALL AND THEN TO HIS SON'S FACE, AND THEN HE HAS A THOUGHT LIKE "EVERYTHING IS A LIE," OR "HOW CAN I LIVE IN A WORLD WHERE—"

HEY DO YOU WANT TO PLAY A GAME WITH ME?
YEAH!

AND SO:

OKAY, NOW ATTACK ME.
SOCIETY

AHHHHHHHH!

THERE IS NO WAY TO FIGHT ME!!
I WILL DESTROY YOU!!!
SOCIETY

MR. BABY! WHERE DO WE GO WHEN WE DREAM?!
WHERE DO BABY'S COME FROM?!?
ARE YOU EXCITED TO HAVE BEEN BORN?
I'M NOT EXCITED TO BE ANYTHING

WHAT IS YOUR OPINION OF AMERICA, BABY?
IT IS MY OPINION AMERICA IS A VERY FINE PLACE

AND YOUR FATHER? WHAT IS YOUR OPINION OF HIM?
MY FATHER IS A VERY FINE MAN

BABY! TELL US ABOUT YOUR PROBLEMS!!
YOU WOULDN'T UNDERSTAND
PLEASE TELL US BABY, MAYBE WE CAN HELP!

HOW DO I KNOW YOU PEOPLE CARE ABOUT ME?

YOU DON'T CARE ABOUT ME

DON'T WE BABY?

I WONDER WHAT IT IS YOU PEOPLE WANT FROM ME...

PERHAPS IT ISN'T SO COMPLICATED AS YOU THINK?

... PERHAPS NOT

PERHAPS IT ISN'T NECESSARY TO KNOW ?...

...PERHAPS NOT...

TODAY BABY SKIPS SCHOOL TO READ BOOKS IN THE PARK BY THE PUBLIC LIBRARY
PUBLIC LIBRARY
THE AIR SMELLS SWEET AND THE SPRING SUN STREAMING THROUGH THE SKYLIGHT IN THE FOYER CARRIES WITH IT THE PLEASANT MUSIC OF BIRDS CHIRPING
WHILE BROWSING, ENTIRELY BY ACCIDENT, BABY FINDS HIS FATHER'S BOOK MISTAKENLY SHELVED IN THE SHORT FICTION SECTION
ALWANI
IT WAS HIS FATHER'S FIRST COLLECTION OF SHORT STORIES AND IMMEDIATELY GARNERED HIM INTERNATIONAL CRITICAL ACCLAIM UPON ITS PUBLICATION
HE WOULD HAVE BEEN ONLY A FEW YEARS OLDER THAN ME WHEN HE WROTE THIS
AFTER SETTLING WITH A GINGER SODA AGAINST THE TRUNK OF A CHESTNUT TREE
THE HELL OF LIFE
SAMI ALWANI
"MY JOB IS TO POPULATE THE ENTIRE EARTH WITH LIES IN THE PROCESS OF CONSTRUCTING MY PHILOSOPHY"
-SAMI

SHORTLY AFTERWARDS...

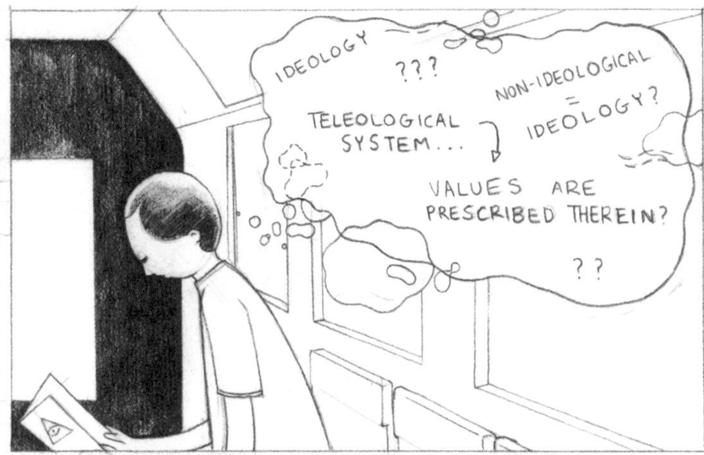
IDEOLOGY
???
NON-IDEOLOGICAL = IDEOLOGY?
TELEOLOGICAL SYSTEM...
VALUES ARE PRESCRIBED THEREIN?
??

ON HIS WAY HOME BABY SEES A WOMAN STUMBLING AND YELLING INSANELY FURTHER UP THE STREET. SHE WALKS SLOWLY TOWARDS AND THEN PAST HIS HOUSE AND BABY SLACKENS HIS PACE IN ORDER TO AVOID CATCHING UP WITH HER

AFTER DINNER BABY APPROACHES HIS FATHER:
I READ YOUR BOOK TODAY, DAD, AND SOME PARTS OF IT CONFUSED ME. THE EVENTS YOU DESCRIBE AFFIRM CERTAIN TRUTHS WHILE NEGATING THEM SIMULTANEOUSLY. IF SOME ASPECTS OF WHAT YOU SAY ARE TRUE THEN OTHER CONTRADICTORY THINGS MUST ALSO BE TRUE. THE VALUES BY WHICH I ORIENT MY UNDERSTANDING OF THE MOST BASIC PHENOMENA ARE SUBVERTED AND REPLACED ONLY WITH A SERIES OF UNANSWERED QUESTIONS.

EVERYTHING GETS TWISTED ROUND, LIKE THE PROGRESS OF A FALLING LEAF.

YOUR TREE LEFT BARE

MAYBE IF YOU DIDN'T TRY TO UNDERSTAND EVERYTHING ALL THE TIME YOU WOULDN'T GET SO FUCKING CONFUSED.
THWUMP!

• • •

WHAT IS YOUR OPINION OF CAPITALISM BABY ?

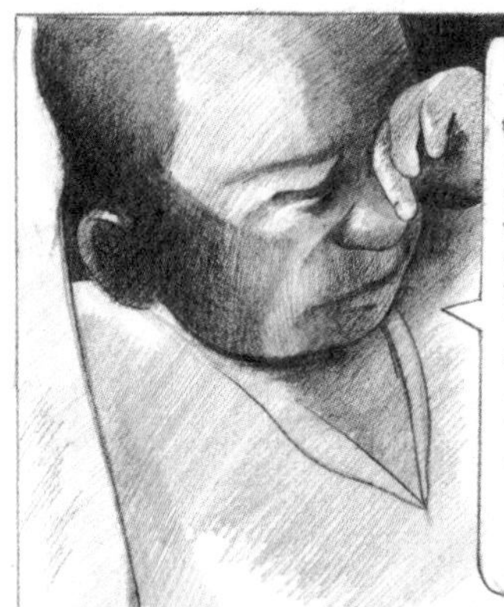
IT IS MY OPINION THAT THE GREATER PORTION OF A MAN'S LIFE SHOULD BE DEDICATED TO THE PURSUIT OF CAPITAL AND PROPERTY AND THAT IN HIS ENDEAVORS WITH HIS FELLOW MAN THIS PURSUIT SHOULD BE HELD AHEAD OF ALL OTHERS IN HIS MIND

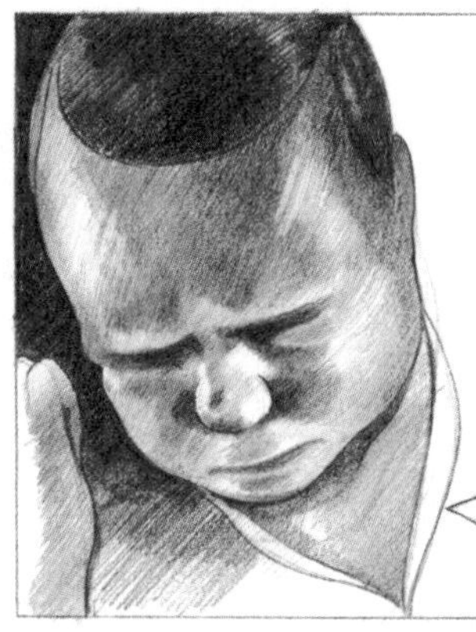
IN THIS LIGHT, THE SOCIAL FOUNDATIONS OF OUR GOVERNMENT AND THE SYSTEMS OF POWER THAT DETERMINE THE WELFARE, HEALTH AND WELLBEING OF ALL THOSE PARTICIPATING IN OUR SOCIETY SHOULD BE DESIGNED SO AS TO PLACE THESE VALUES OF OWNERSHIP AND PROPERTY ABOVE ALL OTHER FORMS OF MEANINGFUL INTERACTION

SO THAT A MAN SHOULD BE ABLE TO JUDGE THE WORTH OF HIS NEIGHBOR ONLY IN TERMS OF HIS USEFULNESS TO HIM IN PRACTICAL EXCHANGE, WHETHER IT BE MONETARY, AN EXCHANGE OF GOODS, OR OF SERVICES RENDERED

IF WE CAN UNCONSCIOUSLY PROJECT THESE SAME METAPHORICAL STRUCTURES OF CAPITAL AND PROPERTY ON THE PSYCHOLOGICAL AND EMOTIONAL EXCHANGES WE MAKE WITH OUR FRIENDS, LOVED ONES, WIVES AND CHILDREN, WE CAN ONLY EXPECT TO SEE GROWING PROSPERITY AND GENUINE HAPPINESS IN ALL PARTS OF OUR LIVES

• • •

Z Z Z Z Z...
BABY WATCHES INTENTLY AS HIS FATHER'S PALID EYELIDS FLUTTER AND FINALLY FALL, THE BRITTLE GLASS OF BABY'S SNIFTER PRESSED AGAINST HIS SHIVERING TEETH

THROUGH SPASMODIC BREATH HE SWALLOWS THE LAST LONG DRAUGHTS OF HIS DRINK
AND THOUGH ANXIETY SEIZES HIS HEART LIKE THE CLAWS OF A VULTURE, HE TAKES GREAT CARE TO PLACE THE GLASS AS SILENTLY AS POSSIBLE ON THE WOODEN TABLE AS HE RISES FROM HIS SEAT

IN A CRAWLSPACE UNDER THE BASEMENT STAIRS BY THE FAINT MOONLIGHT WANING THROUGH A SMALL WINDOW, BABY CONTINUES HIS LETTER...

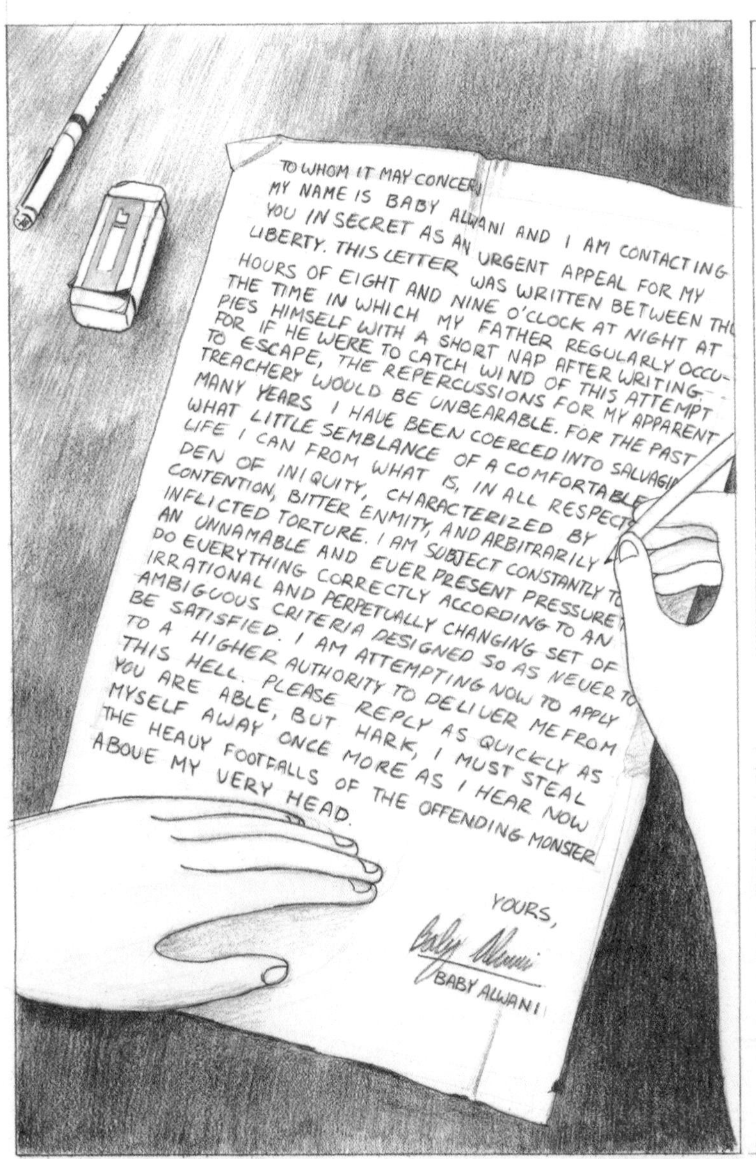

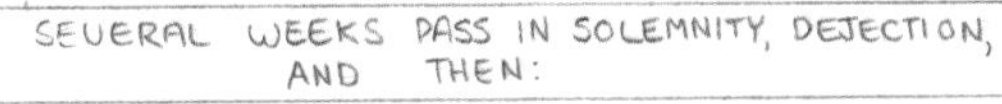

THE HIGH COURT, UPON THE INTERVENTION OF AN INFLUENTIAL PERSON, HAS DISMISSED YOUR SUIT OUT OF HAND

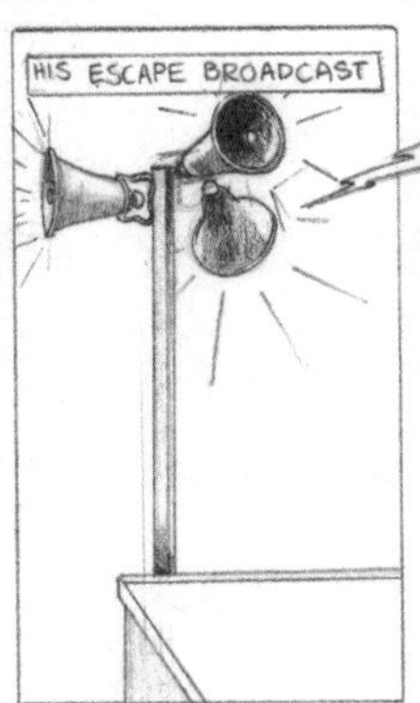

OVER MOUNTAINS...

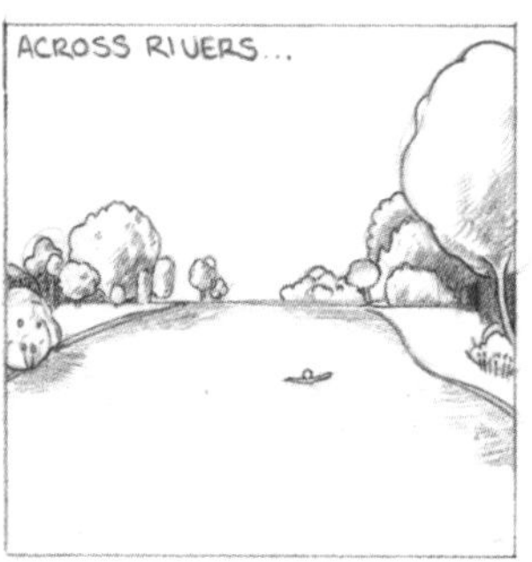
ACROSS RIVERS...

THROUGH DESERTS...

BABY, AS IF FROM A GREAT DISTANCE NOW, REALIZES HE IS FREEZING COLD

A THICK BLACK BLANKET SPREADS ACROSS HIS BRAIN AND HE FALLS ASLEEP

IN HIS SLUMBER HE IS CAPTURED AND RETURNED TO HIS FATHER

• • •

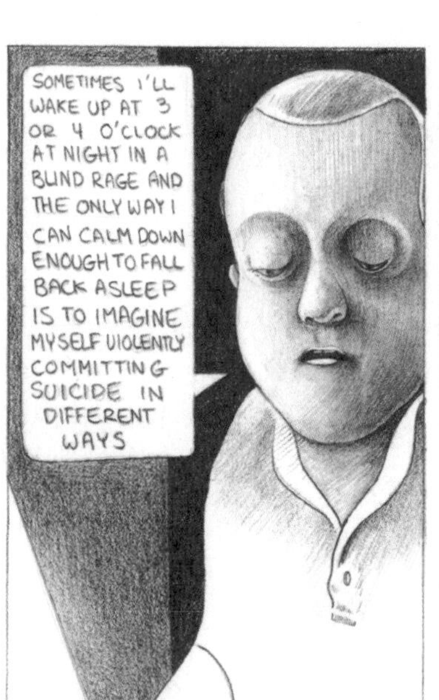
SOMETIMES I'LL WAKE UP AT 3 OR 4 O'CLOCK AT NIGHT IN A BLIND RAGE AND THE ONLY WAY I CAN CALM DOWN ENOUGH TO FALL BACK ASLEEP IS TO IMAGINE MYSELF VIOLENTLY COMMITTING SUICIDE IN DIFFERENT WAYS

HANGING

BREAKING A BOTTLE OVER MY HEAD

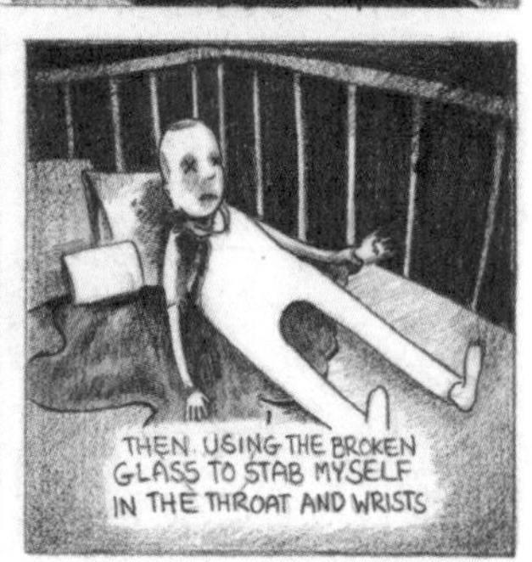
THEN USING THE BROKEN GLASS TO STAB MYSELF IN THE THROAT AND WRISTS

IT'S AS THOUGH MY FACULTIES FOR SELF-WORTH AND MY SENSE OF CONFIDENCE IN THE VALIDITY OF MY ACTIONS AND THE COURSE OF MY LIFE HAVE SUFFERED A SUB-TERRANEOUS SEA-CHANGE IMBUING ME WITH A PRETERNATURAL CAPACITY FOR SELF-LOATHING

LIKE SOME UNPITEOUS MIRROR HELD UP TO MY HISTORY...

REVEALING EVEN MY HAPPIEST MOMENTS AS SOME TRIFFLING AND IRREDEEMABLE NAIEVITE

• • •

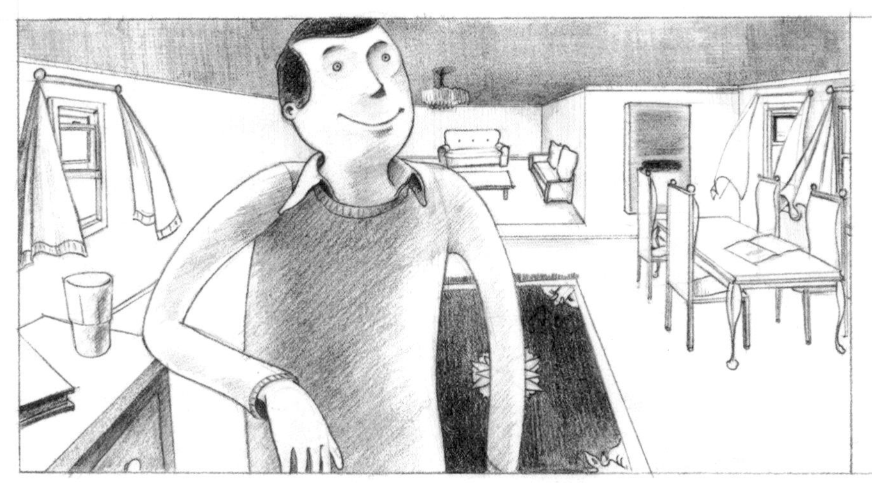

THROUGH A COMBINATION OF SAMI'S CONTINUOUS CHAIN SMOKING AND THE MELANCHOLY STALE HUMORS PRODUCED BY DEPRESSION AND ALCOHOLISM, A HAUNTING STILLNESS HAD BEEN ACCUMULATING IN THEIR SHARED LIVING QUARTERS FOR THE PAST MANY WEEKS. NOTICING THE MILD AND PLEASANT WEATHER ON THE MORNING OF HIS FATHER'S DEPARTURE FOR AN IMPORTANT BUSINESS TRIP, BABY OPENED ALL THE WINDOWS IN THE HOUSE IN AN EFFORT TO CLEAR THE STAGNANT AIR. FOR THE COURSE OF THE FEW REMAINING DAYLIGHT HOURS, THE ROOMS SEEMED TO SWIM IN AN INTOXICATING CLARITY AND FRESHNESS THAT BABY FOUND AGREEABLE, THOUGH FOREIGN AND UNFAMILIAR

. . .

"AH, WHAT PLEASANT CLIMES, SO STRANGE AND NEW TO MY SENSES"

BABY SPENDS THE REST OF THE MORNING ENTERTAINING HIMSELF WITH A BOOK OF SHORT STORIES AND A SMALL POT OF COFFEE ON THE BALCONY. THE SPACE OF A FEW HOURS SEEMS TO DISSOLVE INTO AN EASY REVERIE, AND UPON REACHING ITS CONCLUSION, BABY PUTS THE BOOK DOWN WITH THE FEELING THAT SOME INVISIBLE CONFLICT HAS BEEN RESOLVED IN HIS MIND. INSPIRED BY THE ENCOURAGING PROGRESS OF THE DAY'S EVENTS, HE RESOLVES TO PHONE OVER AN INTIMATE FRIEND AND FOR A SHORT PERIOD OF UNBROKEN BLISS, THE TWO LOVERS LANGUOR IN EACH OTHER'S ARMS

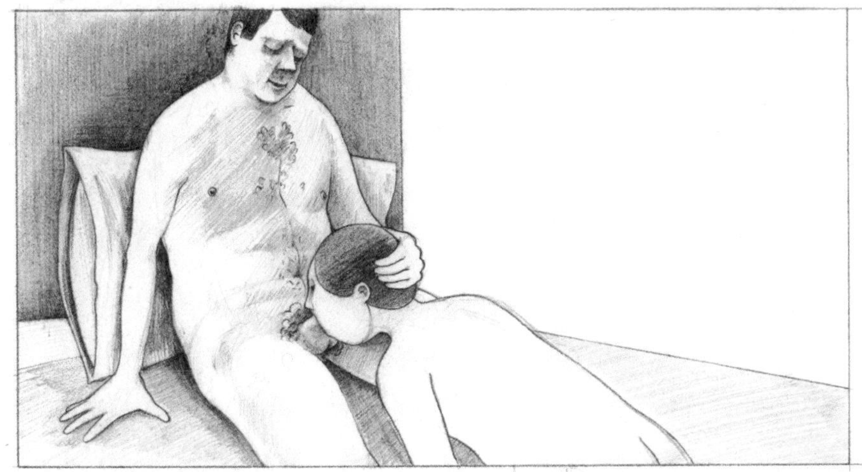

VERY SHORTLY AFTER ENJOYING EACH OTHER'S INTIMATE COMPANY, BABY'S BOYFRIEND RECEIVES A SUMMONS BY TELEPHONE AND IS FORCED TO TAKE LEAVE FOR AN UNEXPECTED REASON. BABY MAKES A VAGUE ATTEMPT TO CONCEAL HIS DISAPPOINTMENT AND ALTHOUGH HIS INTERIOR HEARTBREAK IS OBVIOUS, THE URGENCY OF THE SUMMONS REQUIRES HIS FRIEND'S IMMEDIATE ATTENTION AND THE MAN LEAVES WITHOUT FURTHER DELAY

UPON HIS PARTNER'S DEPARTURE BABY SEEMS UNUSUALLY CALM, BUT IN NOT MORE THAN A FEW MINUTES HE BEGINS CONSIDERING THE IRONY OF HIS HAVING AIRED THE HOUSE EARLIER IN THE DAY ONLY TO FIND THE FRESH AIR NOW SUBSTITUTED WITH THE SICKLY SWEET AROMA OF HIS ABSENT LOVER. THEN, AS QUICKLY AS THE WINTER SUN FALLS IN THE SKY, THE DEEP PARALYSIS OF DEPRESSION BEGAN TO SETTLE OVER HIM. BABY HAD BEEN LOST IN A PARADE OF SELF-PITYING FANTASIES FOR THE PAST QUARTER HOUR WHEN THE PHONE RINGS WITH BABY'S BEAU

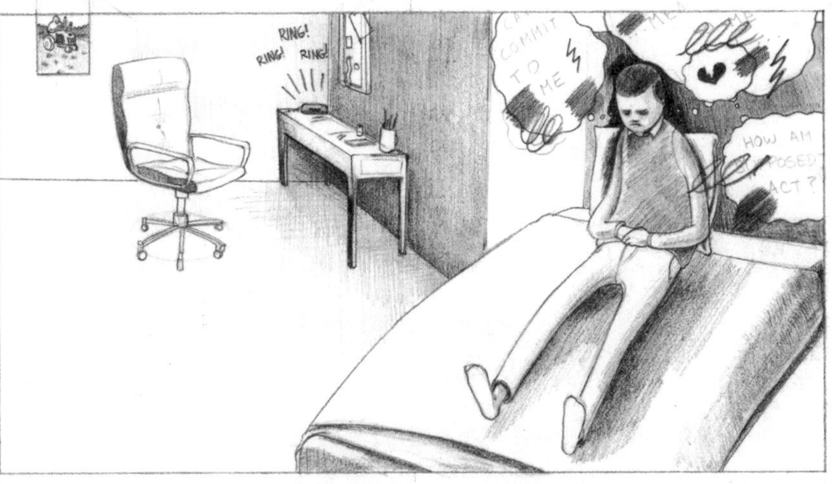

"LEFT <u>CHOKING</u> ON THE <u>AIR</u> STILL <u>THICK</u> WITH YOUR <u>SCENT</u>!!"

• • •

AT FIRST BABY'S RESPONSE IS BITTER REPROACH, BUT SLOWLY IT BECOMES OBVIOUS THAT THE ENGAGEMENT THAT DREW BABY'S FRIEND AWAY THAT EVENING REALLY WAS UNAVOIDABLE, AND EVEN BABY HAS TO CONCEDE THAT IN LIEU OF THE CIRCUMSTANCES, HE DID EVEN MORE FOR BABY THAN COULD HAVE BEEN EXPECTED OF HIM. BABY HANGS UP THE TELEPHONE FEELING NOT HAPPY OR SAD

IN THE EVENING BABY TAKES A WALK DOWN TO THE HARBOR, A SHORT DISTANCE FROM HIS HOUSE, AND BACK. THE CHILL IN THE AIR, AND THE DARKNESS, SEEM TO RECAST THE STREETS INTO AN INFINITY OF MALLEABLE REALITIES AND OVER EACH PASSING FACE BABY FINDS HIMSELF PROJECTING THE POSSIBILITY OF A PASSIONATE AND ELABORATE RELATIONSHIP EXTENDING OVER MANY YEARS AND ENCOMPASSING A VARIETY OF POSITIVE AND NEGATIVE EXPERIENCES

FOR A MOMENT THESE FANTASIES SEEM TO POSSESS A SUPERNAL LUSTER, BUT AS BABY FOLLOWS EACH THREAD TO ITS CONCLUSION, HE FINDS THEM ALL INVARIABLY COLLAPSE INTO THE SAME DULL, MATTE EMOTIONAL ABSENCE THAT WEAVES THROUGH ALL HIS EXPERIENCES AND OCCUPIES AND PERMEATES HIS BODY EVEN NOW, LIKE A MALEVOLENT PHANTOM AS HE REENTERS THE HOUSE

• • •

THE EVENING CONCLUDES WITH NOTHING ELSE FURTHER TO NOTE AND BABY WAKES UP THE NEXT MORNING FEELING MAYBE DIFFERENT, MAYBE HAPPIER, BUT DOUBTING HOW LONG THIS FEELING WILL LAST

• • •

YOU ARE RESP-ONSIBLE!!
I AM IMPLICATING YOU!!
IT IS YOUR RESPONSIBILITY TO SEE!! LIKE I DO SEE!!

A DARKNESS FALLS ACROSS SAMI'S FACE AS HE LIFTS THE BABY FROM ITS CRIB

WELL, IT SEEMS IT'S ABOUT TIME FOR BABY'S NAP
UNFORTUNATELY, I'LL HAVE TO BRING THIS INTERVIEW TO A CLOSE

BUT PAPA!! I AM NOT TIRED!
SAMI MUFFLES THE BABY

HAVE A PLEASANT EVENING EVERYONE

END

[Sonnet] You jerk you didn't call me up

You jerk you didn't call me up

I spent almost a hundred bucks

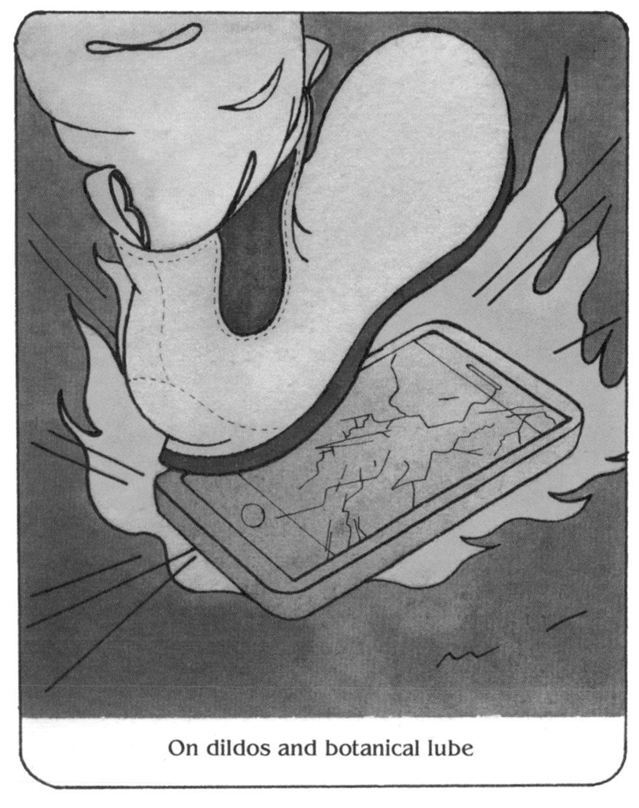

On dildos and botanical lube

So I could fuck myself, while you observe White-Faced

Capuchins from a luxe AirB&B

Treefort in Costa Rica

You could have sent me home with the extra empanadas

At the very least, it was my birthday – are you okay

With a chaste home foot spa and Disney+

I can't offer you an RRSP, real estate

Or Hamilton tickets, but every

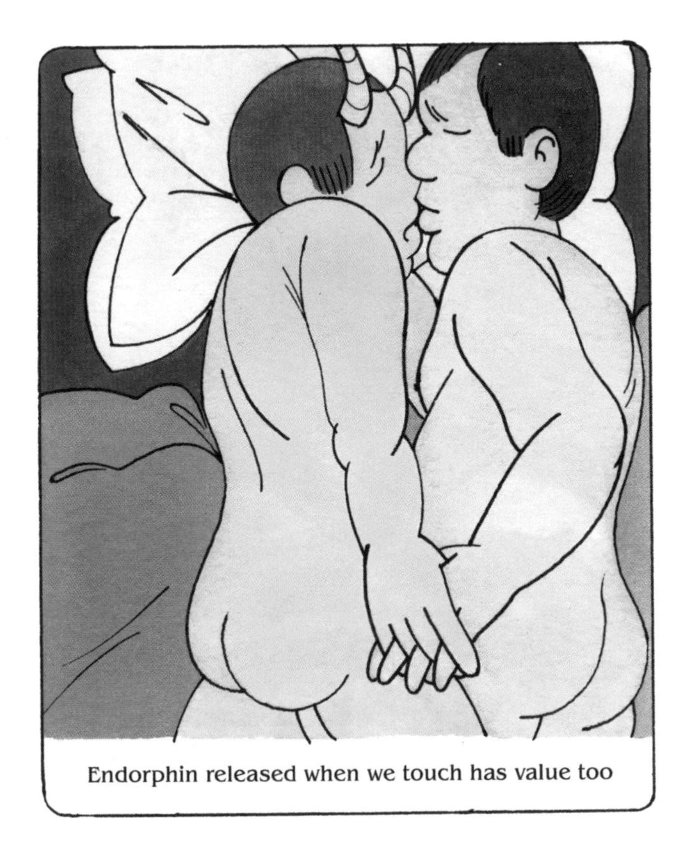

Endorphin released when we touch has value too

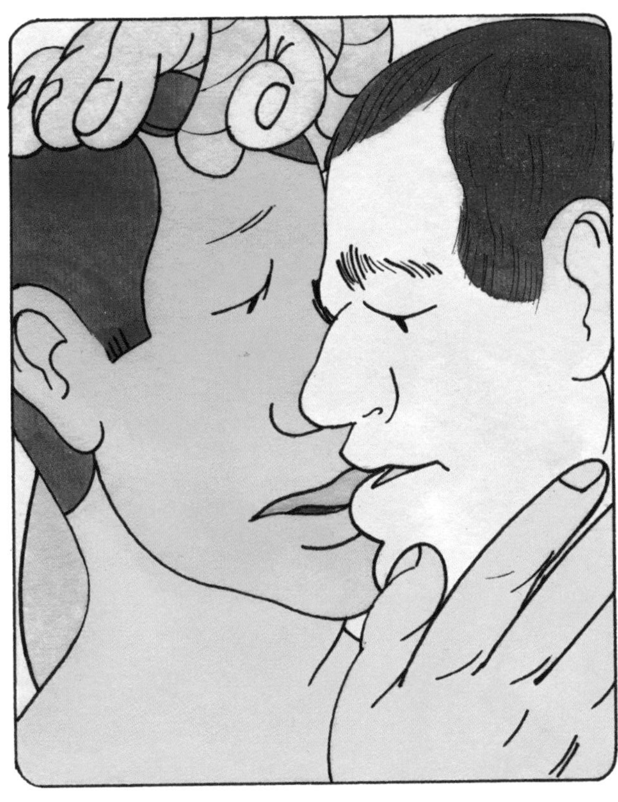

Wake up! It's the middle of the night

You can either make love or freeze
in Arendelle's perpetual winter

Adapted from the poem "(Sonnet) You jerk you didn't call me up" by Bernadette Mayer

E FIRST SIMILARITY I SHARE WITH
THAT WE ARE BOTH FROM
BUT
WAS RAISED BY HIS BIOLOGICAL PARENTS, WHEREAS MY "PARENTS" FOUND ME WHEN I WAS SWAPPED AT BIRTH WITH AN IDENTICAL CHILD I'D SHAPESHIFTED INTO
O BE HONEST, MOST OF MY CHILDHOOD APPEARS
A BLUR TO ME UNTIL THE DAY I MEET
TODAY!
A MOTIVATIONAL LECTURE SERIES IS BEING HELD AT MY HIGH-SCHOOL,
IS ONE OF THE GUEST SPEAKERS
HE TALKS ELOQUENTLY ON A NUMBER OF SUBJECTS, AFTER THE LECTURE I FLOAT THROUGH THE REMAINDER OF MY CLASSES IN A DAZE
ER DURING CLASS ONE OF MY TEACHERS MENTIONS A STORY THAT
MY CONFUSED STATE SEEMS TO HAVE SPECIAL SIGNIFICANCE TO ME
IN THE STORY A MAN SELLS HIS SOUL TO THE DEVIL IN EXCHANGE FOR UNLIMITED POWER

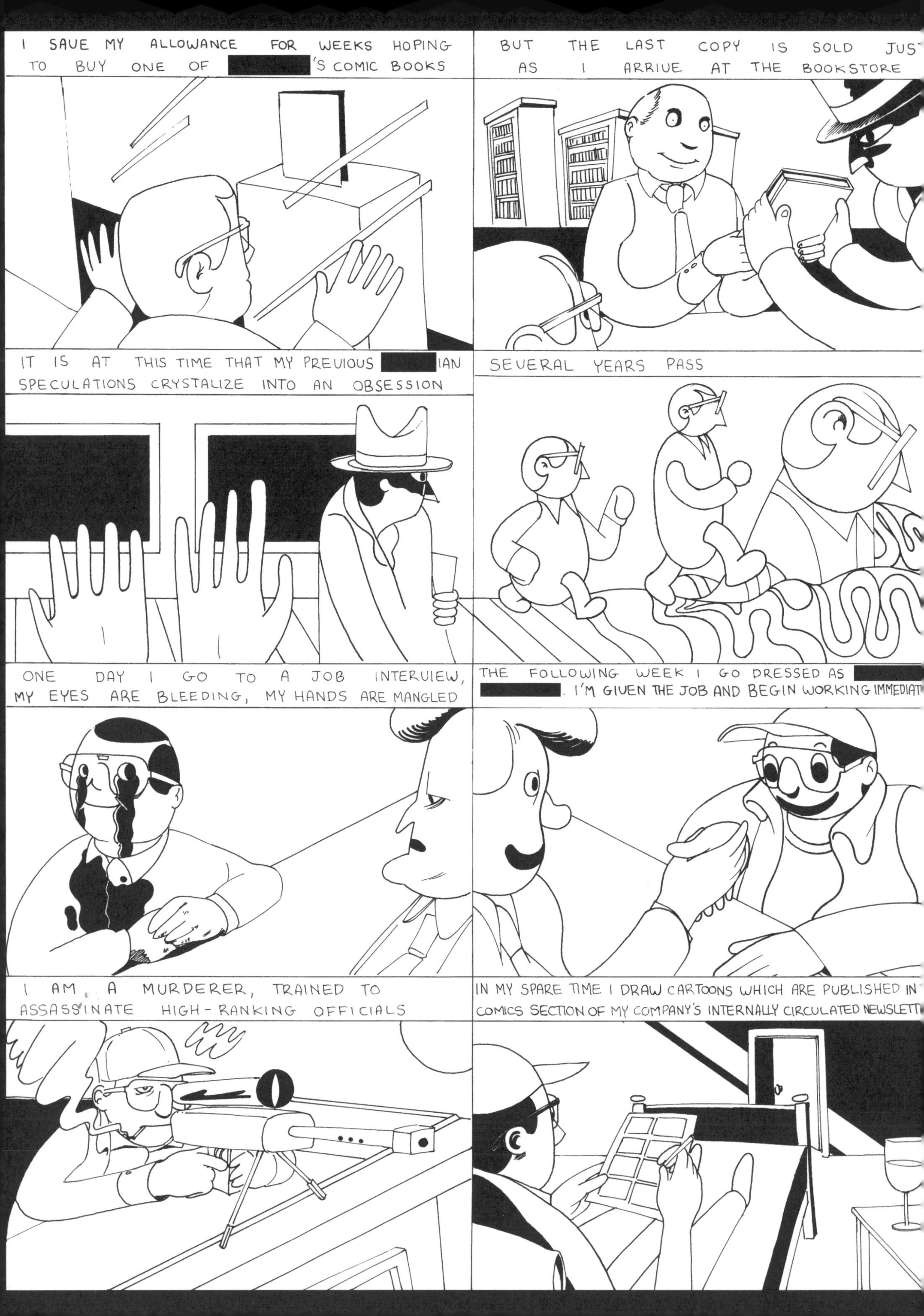
I SAVE MY ALLOWANCE FOR WEEKS HOPING TO BUY ONE OF 's COMIC BOOKS
BUT THE LAST COPY IS SOLD JUST AS I ARRIVE AT THE BOOKSTORE
IT IS AT THIS TIME THAT MY PREVIOUS IAN SPECULATIONS CRYSTALIZE INTO AN OBSESSION
SEVERAL YEARS PASS
ONE DAY I GO TO A JOB INTERVIEW, MY EYES ARE BLEEDING, MY HANDS ARE MANGLED
THE FOLLOWING WEEK I GO DRESSED AS . I'M GIVEN THE JOB AND BEGIN WORKING IMMEDIAT
I AM A MURDERER, TRAINED TO ASSASSINATE HIGH-RANKING OFFICIALS
IN MY SPARE TIME I DRAW CARTOONS WHICH ARE PUBLISHED IN
COMICS SECTION OF MY COMPANY'S INTERNALLY CIRCULATED NEWSLETT

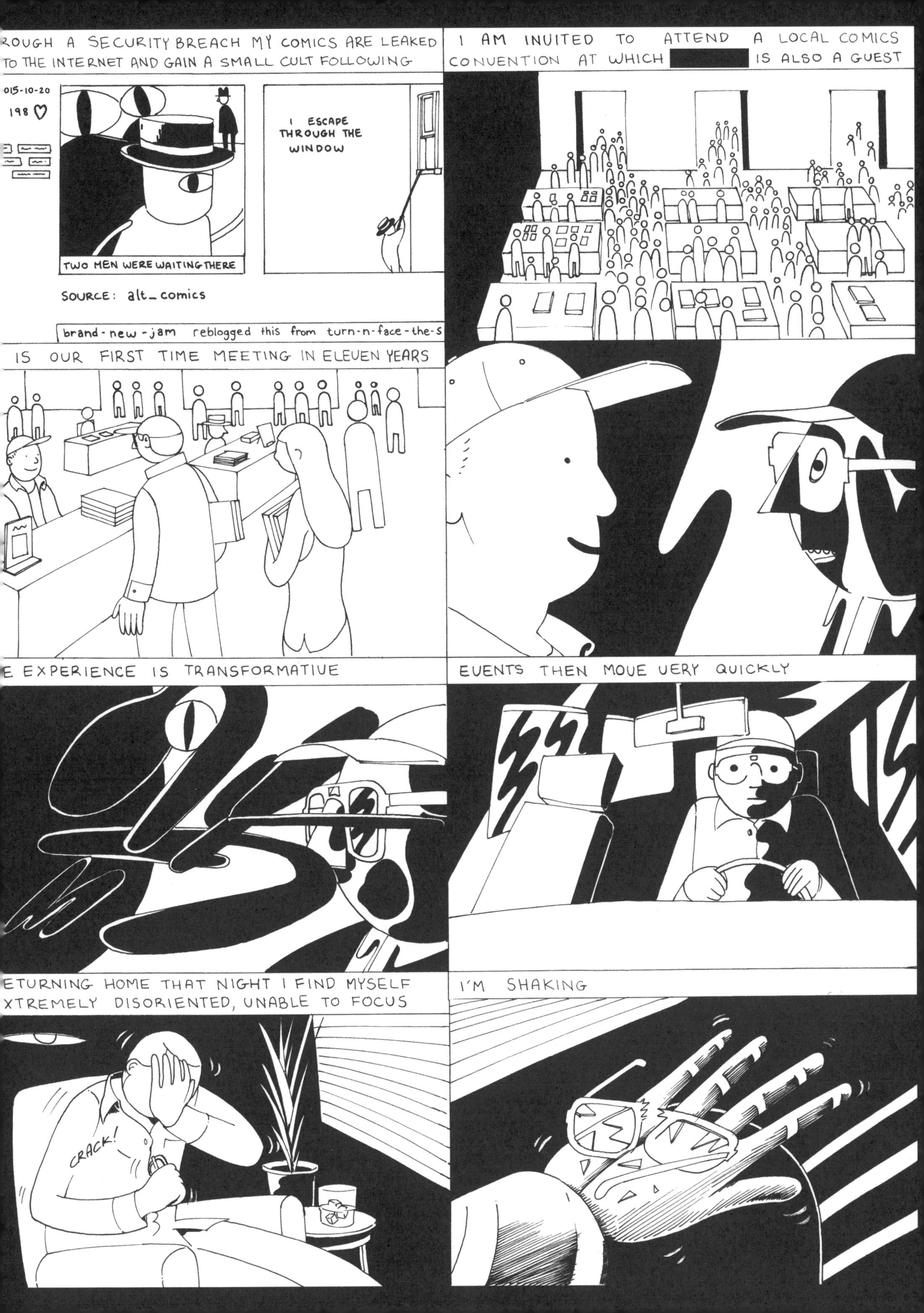
ROUGH A SECURITY BREACH MY COMICS ARE LEAKED TO THE INTERNET AND GAIN A SMALL CULT FOLLOWING
015-10-20
198
TWO MEN WERE WAITING THERE
I ESCAPE THROUGH THE WINDOW
SOURCE: alt_comics
brand-new-jam reblogged this from turn-n-face-the-s
I AM INVITED TO ATTEND A LOCAL COMICS CONVENTION AT WHICH IS ALSO A GUEST
IS OUR FIRST TIME MEETING IN ELEVEN YEARS
E EXPERIENCE IS TRANSFORMATIVE
EVENTS THEN MOVE VERY QUICKLY
ETURNING HOME THAT NIGHT I FIND MYSELF XTREMELY DISORIENTED, UNABLE TO FOCUS
CRACK!
I'M SHAKING

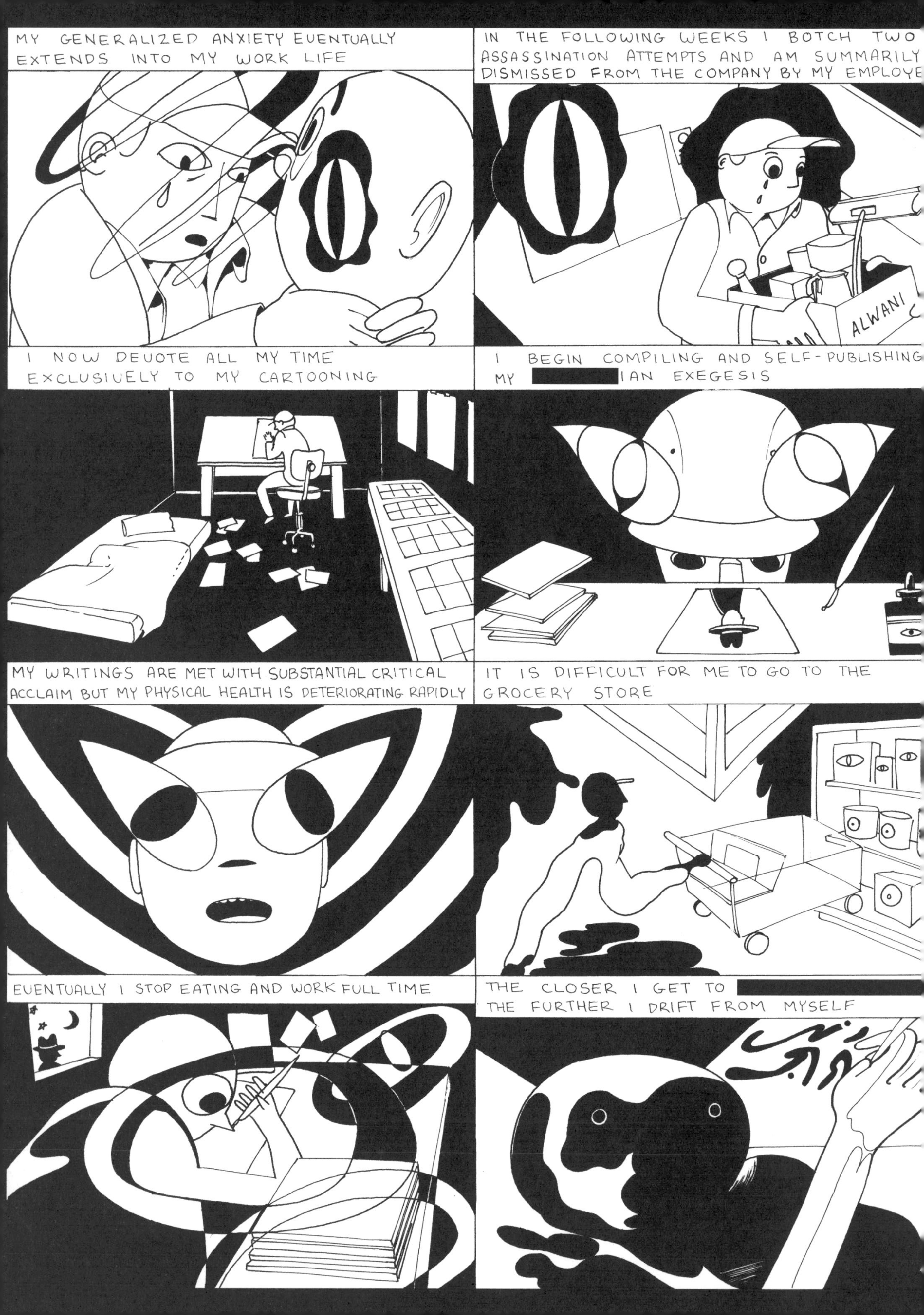
MY GENERALIZED ANXIETY EVENTUALLY EXTENDS INTO MY WORK LIFE
IN THE FOLLOWING WEEKS I BOTCH TWO ASSASSINATION ATTEMPTS AND AM SUMMARILY DISMISSED FROM THE COMPANY BY MY EMPLOYE
ALWANI
I NOW DEVOTE ALL MY TIME EXCLUSIVELY TO MY CARTOONING
I BEGIN COMPILING AND SELF-PUBLISHING MY █████ IAN EXEGESIS
MY WRITINGS ARE MET WITH SUBSTANTIAL CRITICAL ACCLAIM BUT MY PHYSICAL HEALTH IS DETERIORATING RAPIDLY
IT IS DIFFICULT FOR ME TO GO TO THE GROCERY STORE
EVENTUALLY I STOP EATING AND WORK FULL TIME
THE CLOSER I GET TO █████ THE FURTHER I DRIFT FROM MYSELF

AM BROUGHT TO TRIAL FOR IDENTITY THEFT
D THEFT OF INTELLECTUAL PROPERTY AND
IS THE JUDGE PRESIDING OVER MY HEARING
MY SENTENCE IS TO FORM AND REFORM HUMAN SYMBOLS UNTIL THE END OF TIME.

LIFE IS SO COMPLICATED

AND THERE ISN'T EVEN ANY WAY OF PROVING ANYTHING EXISTS.

EVEN IF YOU REMAIN IGNORANT COMPLICATED THINGS YOU DON'T UNDERSTAND STILL HAPPEN TO YOU.

SPLAT!
! ?

PERFECT
DAY

COME INTO MY CAR

EMPATHIZE WITH EACH OTHER!

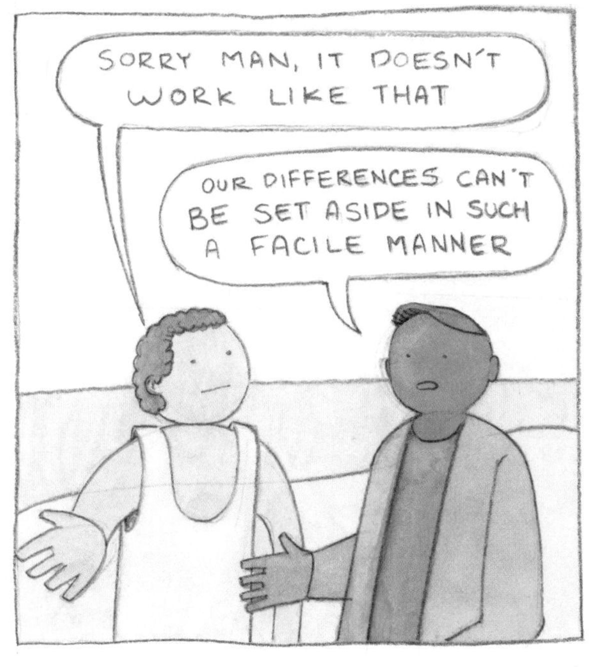

READING WORDSWORTH

TORTURING PEOPLE

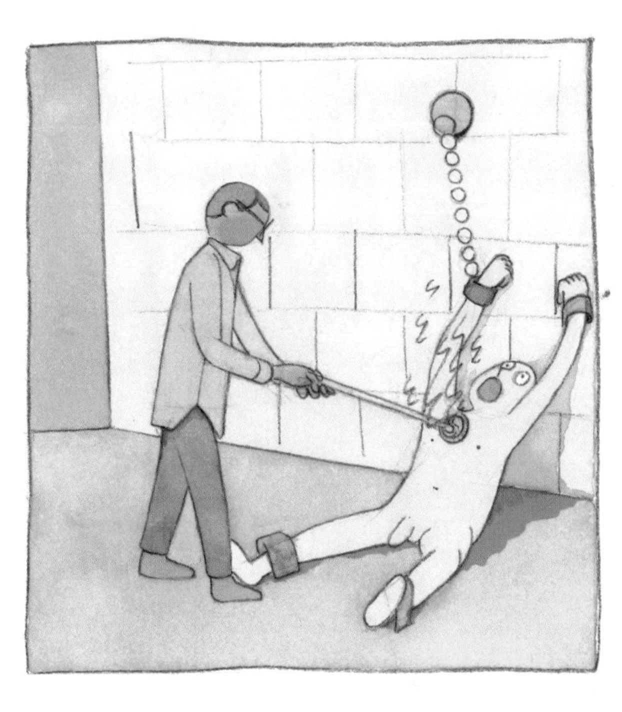

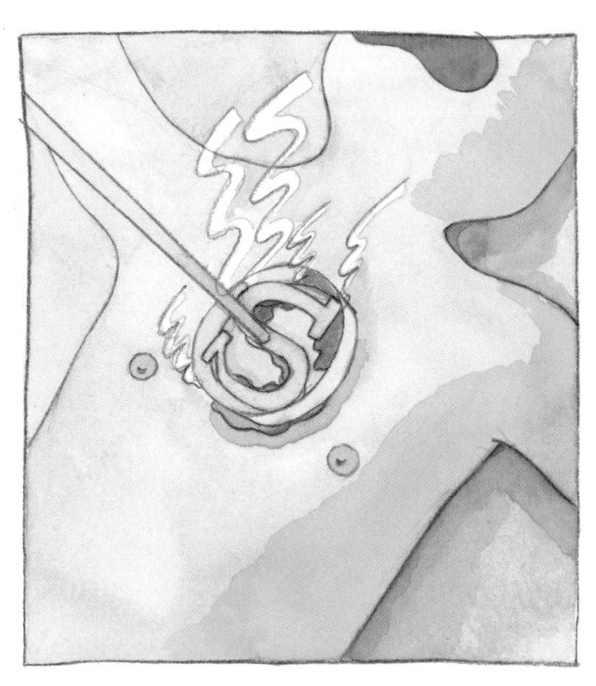

OPEN UP MY SKULL

OPEN UP MY SKULL

LET MY SOUL FLY OUT OF MY BRAIN

UP INTO THE AIR

AND EVAPORATE

Mourning Diary

March 25, 2020

April 10, 2020

YOU KNOW, IN A WAY THE VIRUS REMINDS ME OF MY FATHER!
WON'T LET ME SEE MY FRIENDS! NOT ALLOWED TO SMOKE WEED! NO CASUAL SEX!
DEMOCRACY NOW
• CRISIS DIVIDED ALONG RACIAL ECONOM LINES

Since I'm not going outside I don't need to apply deodorant

But I still do because I crave the oxytocin
ROSE

...and it saves me doing laundry as often

Before isolation I used to dissociate a lot. Strangely, now everything feels completely real.

As if everything's been revealed to be what it's always been

May 3, 2020

Week 7: I have been eating weed every day for 20 days

Recorded audio is now more familiar to me than natural sound

Oprah telecasts at us. "One World."
I WONDER HOW MUCH THE HOUSE SHE'S ZOOMING FROM COSTS?
WOW, IT'S LITERALLY ONE HUNDRED MILLION DOLLARS
...
THAT'S LIKE DR. EVIL MONEY

HOW LONG WOULD IT TAKE ME TO MAKE THAT MUCH?
...
100m / 20k / YEAR =
FIVE THOUSAND YEARS

I've been trying to get along with "The Ghost of Covid-19"
THEY'LL GLADLY SEND US MARCHING TO OUR DEATHS!
FOR AN ECONOMY THAT SERVES NO ONE BUT CRIMINALS!
THE DECADENCE PRODUCED BY A SYSTEM OF CANNIBALISM
"WHO WOULD BE FREE THEMSELVES MUST STRIKE THE BLOW"

ARGH!
SMASH!

DUDE WHAT THE FUCK?!
OH FUCK OH MY GOD I'M SO SORRY!!

TWIN FLAMES OF RIGHTEOUS ANGER & GRIEF'S SOLEMN PARALYSIS DANCE TOGETHER INSIDE ME

EVEN MY ANIMAL CROSSING CHARACTER'S FACE REGISTERS ONLY PLACID RESIGNATION, I FEEL SO DEAD INSIDE

... I THOUGHT HE WAS DEAD?

March??, 2020

The days are long and short. How many?
. . .

What use is a calendar?

Each day is identical
I DON'T KNOW HOW YOU'RE SO HIGH
HONESTLY THESE COOKIES ARE NOT THAT POTENT

I'M DOING A CURBSIDE PICK-UP RUN, WE NEED:
• A CROCK POT • COOKING THERMOMETER • CANNING JARS • SOY LECITHIN
A "POT CROCK-POT"?
DO YOU WANT ANYTHING?

GET ME A GALLON OF LAVENDER ESSENTIAL OIL
I DON'T THINK IT'S SAFE TO HAVE THAT DIFFUSER ON 24 HOURS A DAY

History is cyclical

Avoid thinking about the present moment
EMPLOYMENT INSURANCE

Don't think about the future
GLOBAL DEPRESSION
SURVEILLANCE DYSTOPIA
CRISIS
FASCISM
TECH PEONAGE
EUGENICS
ALSO STILL CLIMATE CHANGE
CRACK!
OW!

What's left?
BON APPETIT! 1:1 CBD:THC TAHINI WALNUT COOKIES!
EAT YOUR HEART OUT KELIS!

May 23, 2020

Dear Diary I've finally settled into a routine that is giving me some structure...

12:00PM ~ Wake up screaming after 11 hours of sleep
AHH!!

12:30-1:30 ~ Look at Animal Crossing memes in my discover feed on Instagram
HAHA
OH ROALD

1:45 ~ Cry silently in the shower + stretching/shoulder rolls

2:15 ~ Read from Roberto Bolano's 2666
Emilia Mena Mena died in June. Her bod
was found in the illegal dump near Calle Yu
on the way to the Hermanos Corinto brick

3:30 ~ Stare into the void

5:30 ~ Sharpen my guillotine while watching old episodes of Broad City with The Ghost of Covid-19
THIS HRC EPISODE IS CRINGE
TRUE, LET'S SKIP THIS ONE

7:00 ~ Police my neighbors by posting photos of them on walks taken from my window to social media
#BUSTED
YOU SELFISH FUCKS!
SNAP!

September 8, 2020

I'm still scared of being outside
TOOT!
Hey the five of us are ubering to indoor tapas, hop in!

When I do see friends The Ghost of Covid-19 always tags along
WOW THAT OLDER WOMAN IS WEARING A MASK, FACE SHIELD AND GLOVES JUST TO WALK DOWN THE STREET
THIS MUST BE SO SCARY FOR KIDS AT SCHOOL... WAIT, YOUR MOM'S AN E.A. ISN'T SHE? I WONDER HOW SHE'S DOING

I am trying to look at the world in a way that doesn't feel painful
HAW HAW

My new plan is to drown myself in work
IT'S 6 A.M. BUT I FEEL FINE
TIME DOESN'T EXIST ANY WAY - EVERY THING THAT WILL EVER HAPPEN HAS ALREADY OCCURED

I ONLY GOT 3 HOURS SLEEP - BUT I'M NOT TIRED. I'LL JUST KEEP GOING LIKE THIS
!!
HEHE
THEN WAKE UP IN ONE OR TWO YEARS WHEN EVERYTHING WILL BE OOOHH-KAY!

Every day I think about mortality and the end of time
THUMP
OOH... MY HEAD...

How can anything exist which has a beginning or end
CLONK
THUNK
YOWL
I WISH HE WERE A LITTLE QUIETER WITH THAT VIBRATOR

Drunk in Love

I MET Ⓐ & Ⓑ IN NOVEMBER

WHAT DETERMINES WHETHER THE TREES TURN YELLOW OR RED?

I THINK THEY ARE JUST DIFFERENT BREEDS OF MAPLE

Ⓐ & Ⓑ FELL IN LOVE 29 YEARS AGO, IN THE SAME YEAR I WAS BORN. AT THAT TIME Ⓐ WAS MARRIED TO A WOMAN WHO URGED HIM TO JOIN THE CHOIR AT THE CHURCH WHERE Ⓑ WAS CHURCH ORGANIST AND CHOIR MASTER.

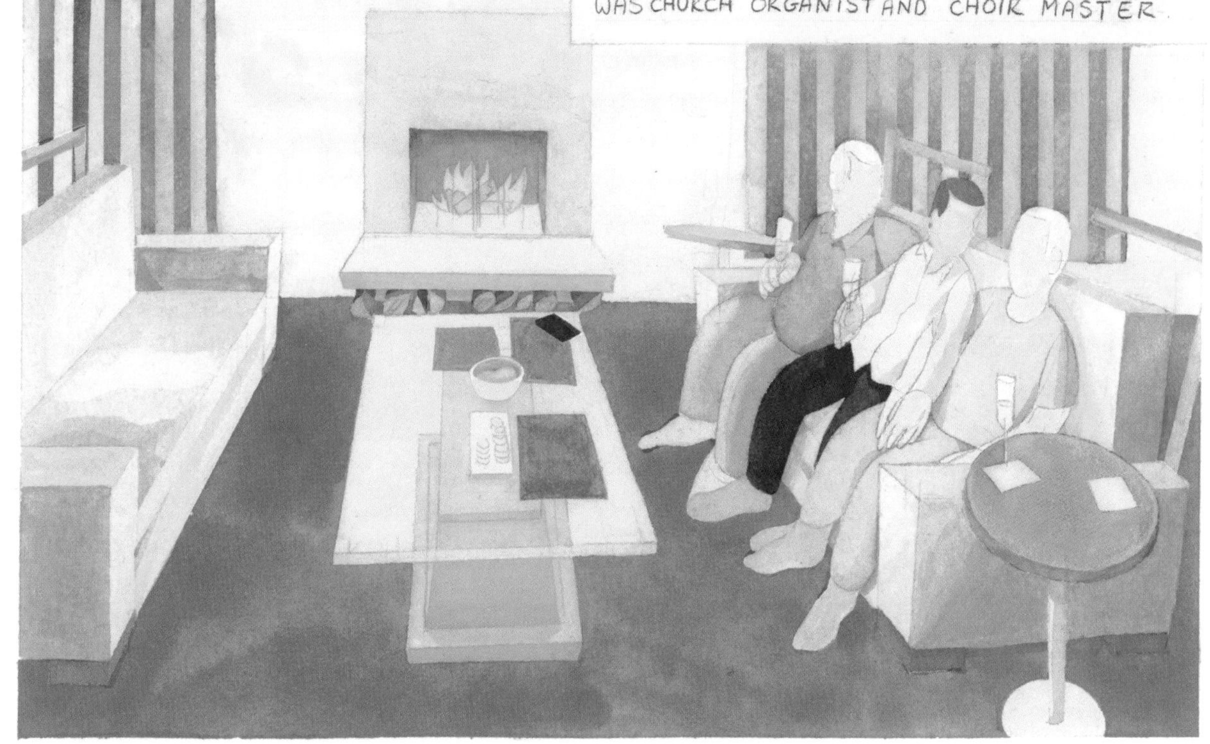

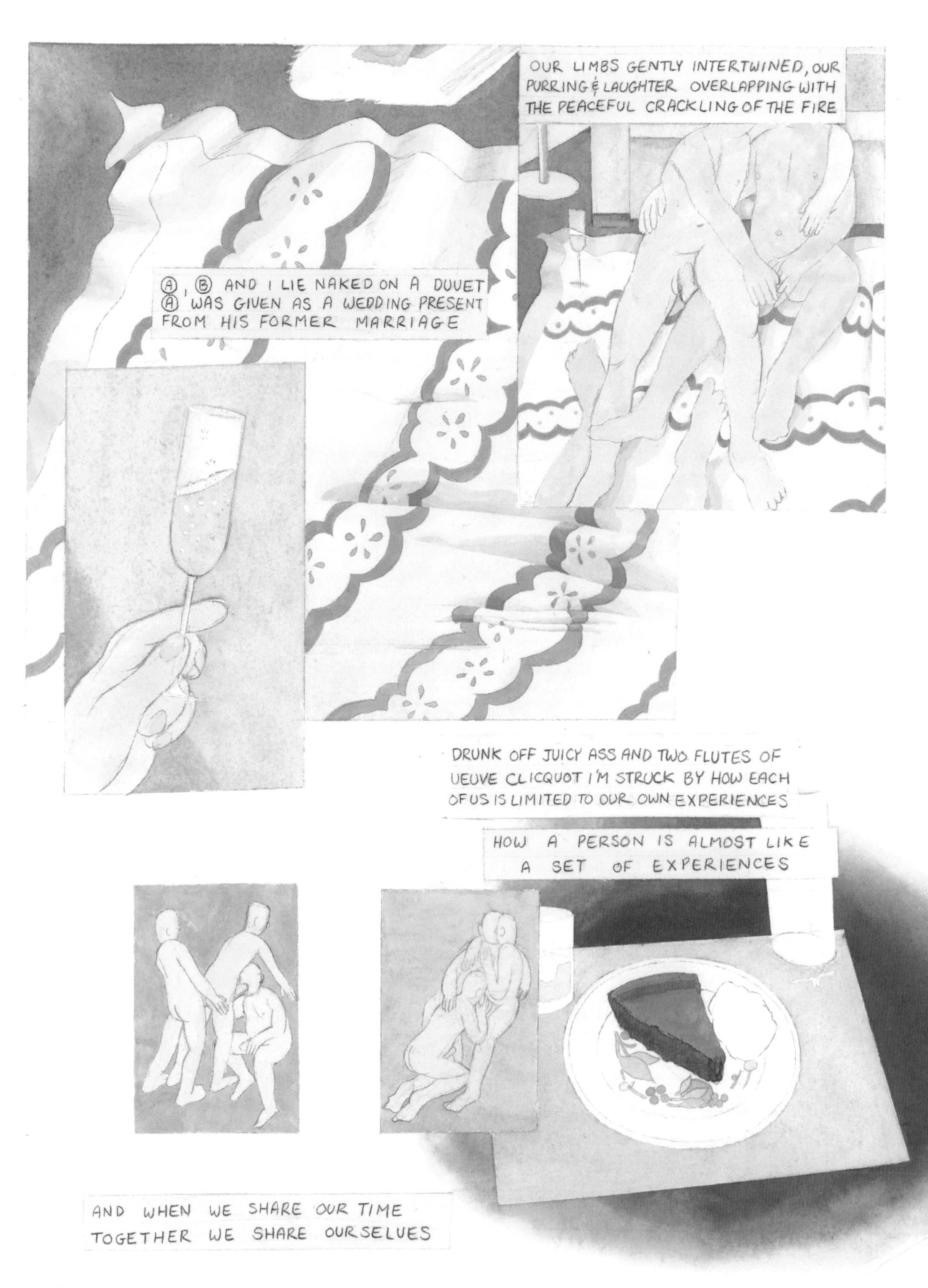
OUR LIMBS GENTLY INTERTWINED, OUR PURRING & LAUGHTER OVERLAPPING WITH THE PEACEFUL CRACKLING OF THE FIRE
Ⓐ, Ⓑ AND I LIE NAKED ON A DUVET Ⓐ WAS GIVEN AS A WEDDING PRESENT FROM HIS FORMER MARRIAGE
DRUNK OFF JUICY ASS AND TWO FLUTES OF VEUVE CLICQUOT I'M STRUCK BY HOW EACH OF US IS LIMITED TO OUR OWN EXPERIENCES
HOW A PERSON IS ALMOST LIKE A SET OF EXPERIENCES
AND WHEN WE SHARE OUR TIME TOGETHER WE SHARE OURSELVES

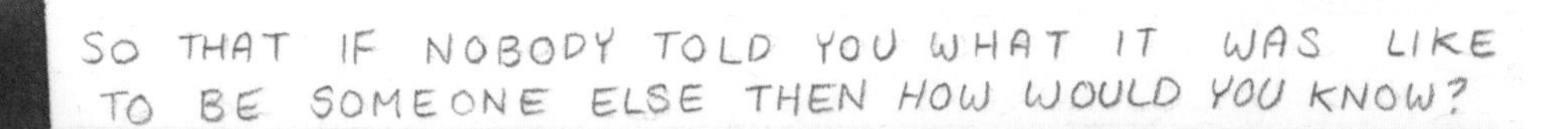

SO THAT IF NOBODY TOLD YOU WHAT IT WAS LIKE TO BE SOMEONE ELSE THEN HOW WOULD YOU KNOW?

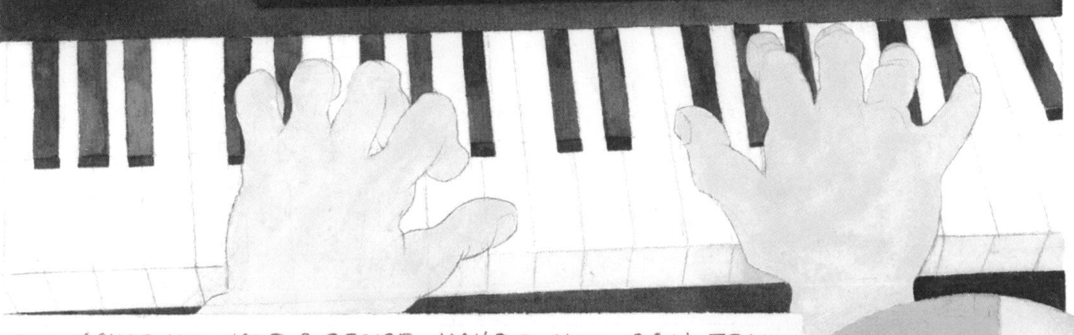

BUT MAYBE YOU HAVE A SENSE, MAYBE YOU CAN TELL WHERE I AM WHEN I'M NOT WITH YOU

BEFORE SEEING Ⓓ THAT NIGHT I ATTENDED A SCREENING OF OSHIMA'S "IN THE REALM OF THE SENSES," WHICH TELLS THE TRUE STORY OF A COUPLE SO SEX OBSESSED THAT ONE ACCIDENTALLY STRANGLES THE OTHER TO DEATH DURING LOVE MAKING

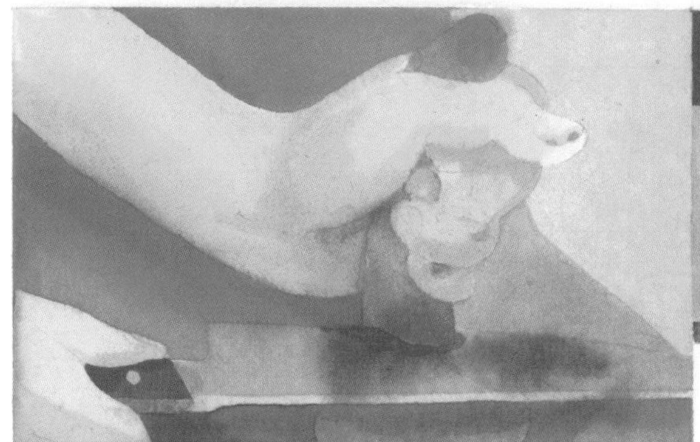

SHE THEN SEVERED THE MAN'S PENIS AND CARRIED IT WITH HER FOR FOUR DAYS

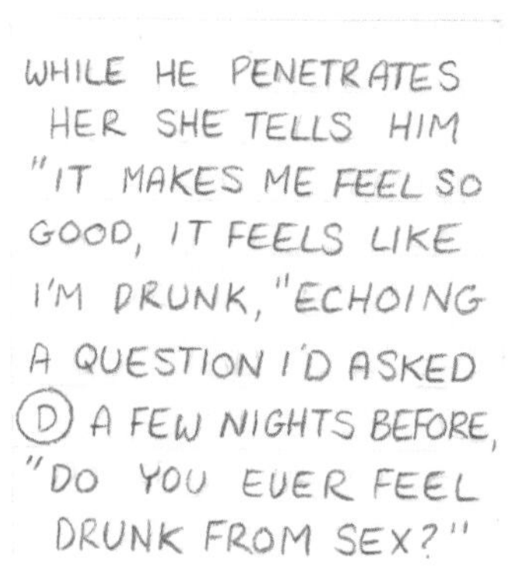

WHILE HE PENETRATES HER SHE TELLS HIM "IT MAKES ME FEEL SO GOOD, IT FEELS LIKE I'M DRUNK," ECHOING A QUESTION I'D ASKED Ⓓ A FEW NIGHTS BEFORE, "DO YOU EVER FEEL DRUNK FROM SEX?"

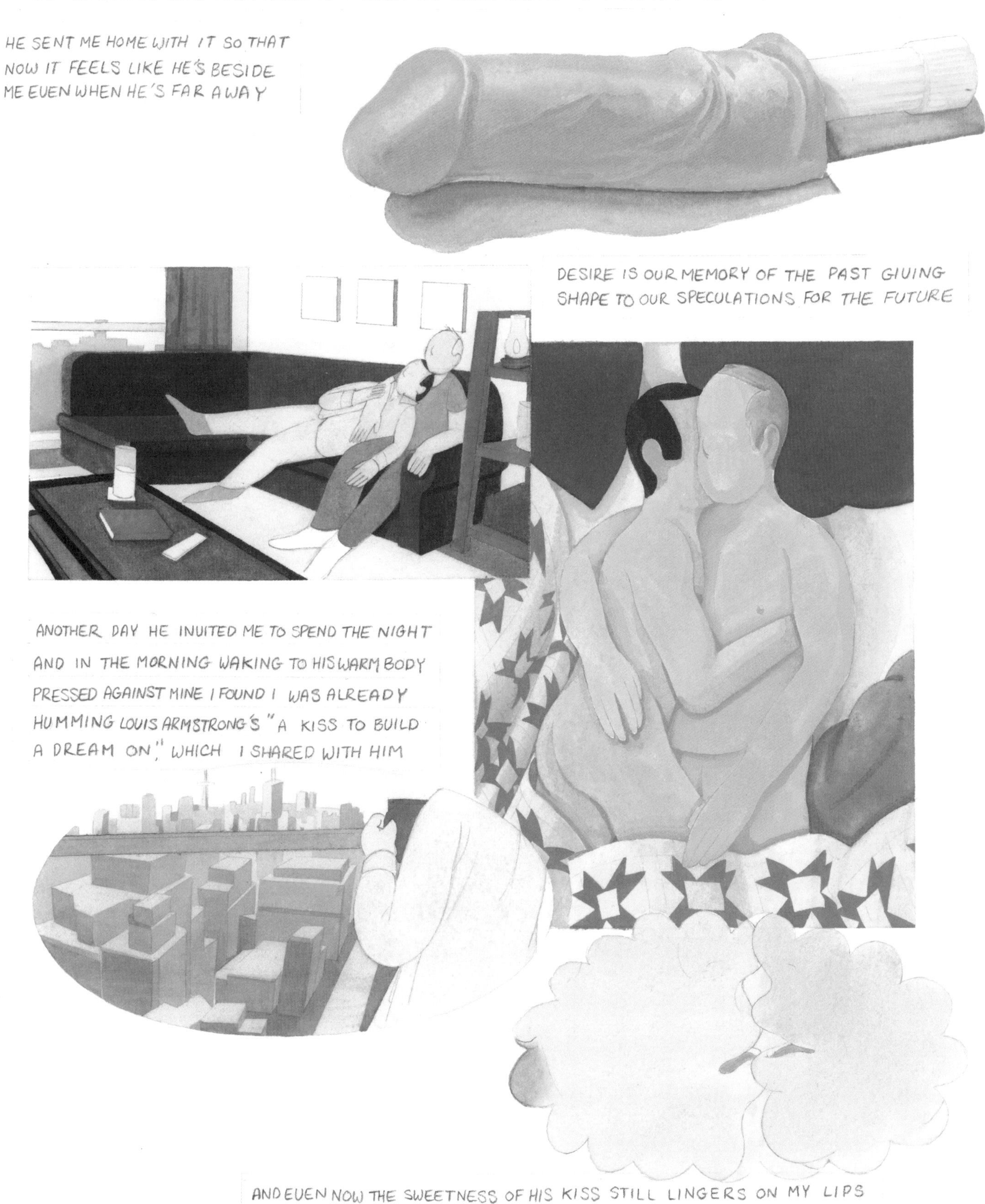
Ⓓ HAD HIS ERECTION CAST INTO A DILDO USING DENTAL ALGENATE & SILICONE. HIS TWIN, THE LIKENESS WAS IDENTICAL AND EVEN CAPTURED THE PERFECT VEINS ON HIS SHAFT
HE SENT ME HOME WITH IT SO THAT NOW IT FEELS LIKE HE'S BESIDE ME EVEN WHEN HE'S FAR AWAY
DESIRE IS OUR MEMORY OF THE PAST GIVING SHAPE TO OUR SPECULATIONS FOR THE FUTURE
ANOTHER DAY HE INVITED ME TO SPEND THE NIGHT AND IN THE MORNING WAKING TO HIS WARM BODY PRESSED AGAINST MINE I FOUND I WAS ALREADY HUMMING LOUIS ARMSTRONG'S "A KISS TO BUILD A DREAM ON," WHICH I SHARED WITH HIM
AND EVEN NOW THE SWEETNESS OF HIS KISS STILL LINGERS ON MY LIPS

I WAS WITH A MAN ONCE WHO TOLD ME HE DIDN'T THINK IT WAS POSSIBLE FOR TWO MEN TO LOVE EACH OTHER. WE HAD BEEN DATING EIGHT MONTHS.

WHAT HAPPENS TO THE LOVE THEN THAT WE BOTH STILL SURELY FEEL

IT GETS SQUASHED INTO SOME SHADOWY COMPARTMENT INSIDE US MAYBE, AND FERMENTS UNTIL IT'S DARK AND STINKS LIKE WHISKEY

AGED 20 YEARS, OR 40 –

AND IT GETS ME DRUNK WHEN I DRINK FROM THE LOVE OF AN OLDER MAN

I DRINK HIS WINE BEFORE I TELL © THAT I SEE US AS ONLY FRIENDS

AND THEN, LIKE HE WAS PUNISHING ME FOR USING HIM WITHOUT HIS PERMISSION, LOUIS ARMSTRONG CAME ON THE RADIO TO SING "CAN'T WE BE FRIENDS," AS Ⓒ & I CLING TOGETHER

MY EYES WANDER, MY EYES ARE BIGGER THAN MY STOMACH, BUT MY TONGUE IS THICK & I'M CONFUSED

HOW CAN ANYONE BE SURE OF WHAT THEY WANT? WHEN Ⓑ PLAYS THE PIANO FOR ME IT SOUNDS SENTIMENTAL AND EXPRESSIVE, WHEN Ⓒ PLAYS EACH NOTE FEELS CONSIDERED AND MEASURED.

Ⓐ AND Ⓑ ARE HUSBANDS, AND Ⓒ DOESN'T WANT A BOYFRIEND, AND Ⓓ HAS A HUSBAND WHO HAS A BOYFRIEND...

AND HOW MANY NOTES AND COMBINATIONS OF NOTES CAN BE PLAYED

IN HOW MANY ARRANGEMENTS, TRANSPOSED TO HOW MANY DIFFERENT OCTAVES

AND HOW MUCH TIME IS THERE IN A DAY?

AND WHERE DOES THE TIME GO AS I WATCH THE LEAVES CHANGE AGAIN, AND THEN WATCH AS THE FROST IS BRUSHED ONTO THE CORNERS OF MY WINDOW?

IS THERE A SONG FOR WHEN I THINK ABOUT FALLING? IN LOVE OR OUT OF THE WINDOW AND ONTO THE STREET? OR A SONG FOR WHEN I DRINK UNTIL I'M DRUNK AND I DON'T KNOW WHAT I WANT OR FROM WHO?

A SONG I HAVEN'T LEARNED TO PLAY BUT SPEND TOO MUCH TIME PLAYING ALREADY

BUT EVERYTHING I'VE JUST WRITTEN I FORGET WHEN I FEEL HIS SKIN CARESS MINE AND TASTE THAT GENTLE ELECTRIC TINGLING ON MY TONGUE AND FEEL IT IN MY HANDS, MY HEART AND MY HEAD LICKED BY THE FLAMES OF AN INTERNAL FIRE

I MEANT FOR THESE DRAWINGS TO BE A GIFT FOR YOU, IN THE SAME WAY I MADE A GIFT FOR SOMEONE ELSE ONCE

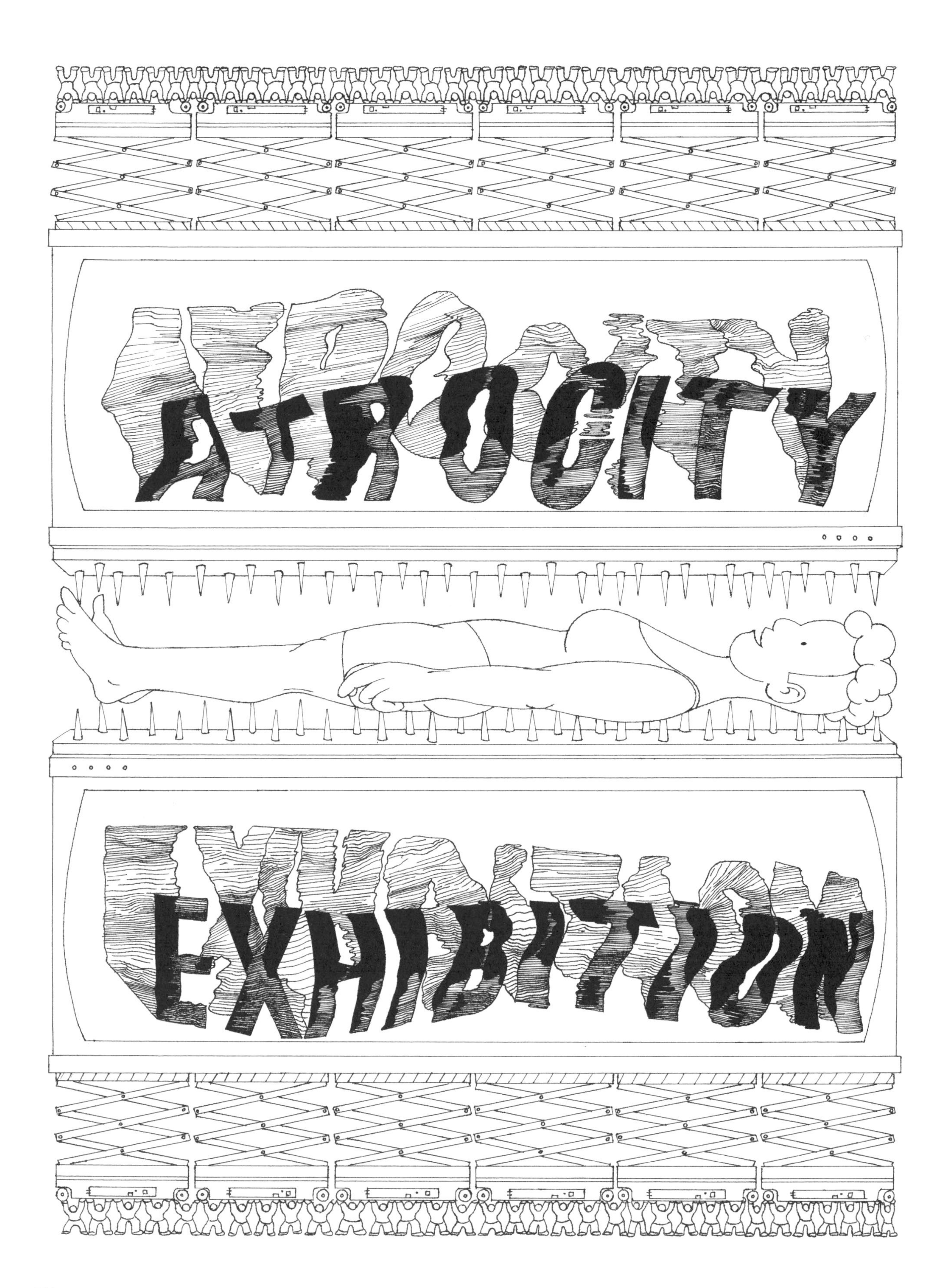
ATROCITY
EXHIBITION

KNOCK KNOCK, GOOD MORNING, WE'RE HERE TO REPOSSESS YOUR HOUSE, YOUR CAR, YOUR JOB, NAME, AND ALL OF YOUR ASSETS AND POSSESIONS
BUT WHY? I'VE DONE NOTHING WRONG I PAY MY BILLS ON TIME

UNFORTUNATELY IT'S ALL ALREADY GONE
BECAUSE IT NEVER BELONGED TO YOU
ARE YOU FAMILIAR WITH PRIMITIVE ACCUMULATION? DO YOU BENEFIT FROM SYSTEMIC VIOLENCE?
I DON'T SEE MYSELF AS A VIOLENT PERSON

DO YOU KNOW ABOUT THE IMF'S* SAPs?**
NO
MAYBE YOU SHOULD MAYBE YOU SHOULD HAVE ALREADY KNOWN
WRETCHED OF THE EARTH
BLACK MARXISM
WOMEN, RACE & CLASS
UNDERS POWER
* INTERNATIONAL MONETARY FUND
** STRUCTURAL ADJUSTMENT PROGRAMS

HERE'S A LIST OF TEXTS TO FAMILIARIZE YOURSELF WITH IF YOU WANT TO UNDERSTAND WHY WE'RE DOING THIS
COMMUNITY HOUSING

FREE
COMMUNIST
Z Z Z Z Z Z Z
SELF
DRIVING
SOLAR TRUCK

WEALTH REDISTRIBUTION CENTER

*BUSINESS IMPROVEMENT AREA

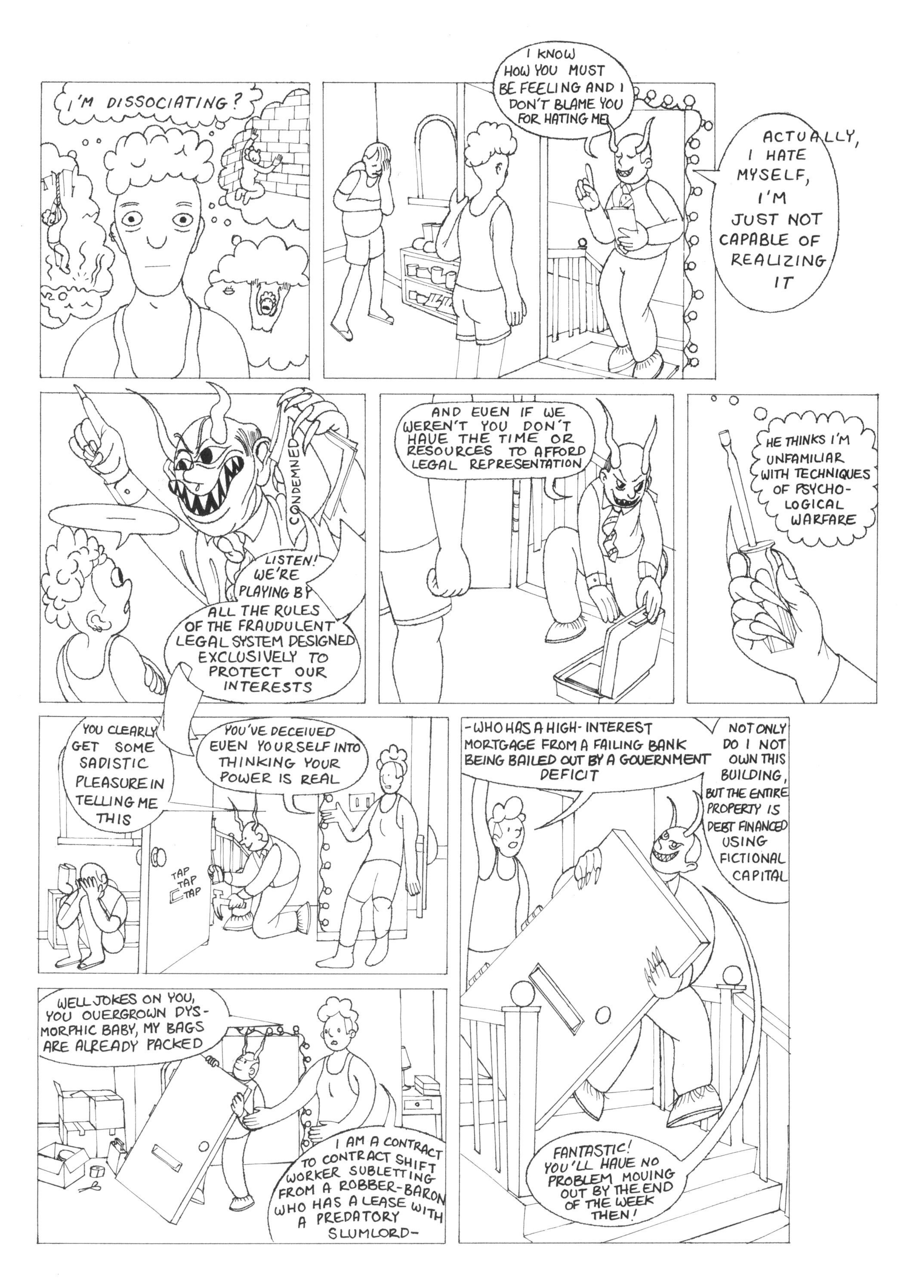
I'M DISSOCIATING?
I KNOW HOW YOU MUST BE FEELING AND I DON'T BLAME YOU FOR HATING ME!
ACTUALLY, I HATE MYSELF, I'M JUST NOT CAPABLE OF REALIZING IT
CONDEMNED
LISTEN! WE'RE PLAYING BY ALL THE RULES OF THE FRAUDULENT LEGAL SYSTEM DESIGNED EXCLUSIVELY TO PROTECT OUR INTERESTS
AND EVEN IF WE WEREN'T YOU DON'T HAVE THE TIME OR RESOURCES TO AFFORD LEGAL REPRESENTATION
HE THINKS I'M UNFAMILIAR WITH TECHNIQUES OF PSYCHO-LOGICAL WARFARE
YOU CLEARLY GET SOME SADISTIC PLEASURE IN TELLING ME THIS
YOU'VE DECEIVED EVEN YOURSELF INTO THINKING YOUR POWER IS REAL
TAP TAP TAP
NOT ONLY DO I NOT OWN THIS BUILDING, BUT THE ENTIRE PROPERTY IS DEBT FINANCED USING FICTIONAL CAPITAL
WELL JOKES ON YOU, YOU OVERGROWN DYS-MORPHIC BABY, MY BAGS ARE ALREADY PACKED
I AM A CONTRACT TO CONTRACT SHIFT WORKER SUBLETTING FROM A ROBBER-BARON WHO HAS A LEASE WITH A PREDATORY SLUMLORD-
-WHO HAS A HIGH-INTEREST MORTGAGE FROM A FAILING BANK BEING BAILED OUT BY A GOVERNMENT DEFICIT
FANTASTIC! YOU'LL HAVE NO PROBLEM MOVING OUT BY THE END OF THE WEEK THEN!

YOU ARE MATERIALLY RICH BUT SPIRITUALLY DESTITUTE!!
NOTHING IS MORE IMPORTANT THAN MY PERSONAL INDIVIDUAL HAPPINESS...
YOUR PROPERTY WILL DESTROY YOU!
UROOM!
YOU OKAY?
SELFISHNESS IS LONELINESS — HOARDING IS ISOLATION
WHAT'S FUNNY IS THIS SOCIETY EXPLOITS EVERYONE FOR THE BENEFIT OF NO ONE
EVEN THE ENSLAVERS SUFFER A SECRET BUT PROFOUND EMPTINESS
I FEEL CRUSHED BY POVERTY BUT WHAT I HATE MORE THAN BEING POOR IS THE SYSTEM THAT KEEPS ME POOR...
— WANT SOME WEED?
SURE
THE POOR ARE TAXED IN ENDLESS WAYS
THE PREDATORY LANDLORDS TIGHTEN THE NOOSE AROUND OUR NECKS
THEN PRECARIOUS EMPLOYMENT KICKS THE STOOL FROM BENEATH OUR FEET...
IT'S OKAY, IT DOESN'T MATTER
IN MY HEAD I'M LIVING IN THE FUTURE
AND WE'VE ALREADY TAKEN EVERY-THING BACK

SYLVIA WHAT'S WRONG?!
ARGH! I'M GETTING ANOTHER OCCULAR MIGRAINE!
MEANWHILE...
AH, FINALLY HOME & SAFE FROM THE PLAGUE RIDDEN MASSES
WHEN MY WEALTH MANAGER WARNED ME ABOUT THE ANCIENT SUPERVIRUS BEING RELEASED FROM THE EARTH'S THAWING PERMAFROST
DECONTAMINATE
I WAS ABLE TO DUMP MY STOCK BEFORE THE MARKET CRASHED THEN BUY THIS ESTATE IN THE COUNTRY FOR A PITTANCE!
MY BEAUTIFUL WIFE, KAREN
PACK YOUR BAGS KEN! OUR FLIGHT IS WAITING
VACATION? BUT I THOUGHT FLIGHTS WERE GROUNDED WHILE THE FACTORY WORKERS WERE STILL OCCUPYING THE AIRPORT IN PROTEST OF THEIR UNPAID WAGES
JUST LAST WEEK THEY WERE STREAMING THE PUBLIC EXECUTION OF THEIR COMPANY'S ED* ON IG** LIVE
LIVE
* EXECUTIVE DIRECTOR
** INSTAGRAM

DON'T WORRY- OUR PRIVATE JET IS ALREADY PARKED ON THE ROOF GARDEN
I EVEN HAD OUR LABRADOR RETRIEVER AND HIS RMT* FLOWN IN FROM THE PET SPA IN MALTA!
FACETIME
*REGISTERED MASSAGE THERAPIST
A FAMILY REUNION!
EXCEPT FOR OUR SON WHO REFUSES TO COME
EVER SINCE HE STARTED SOLICITING THAT GFE* DOMINATRIX FOR EQUITY TRAINING HE DOESN'T LISTEN TO A WORD I SAY ...
*GIRLFRIEND EXPERIENCE
HE JUST SITS IN HIS ROOM FOR HOURS LISTENING TO ROBIN KELLEY LECTURES AND DRAWING HIS "ANTIFA" ILLUSTRATIONS
YOUTUBE
La Croix
THERE THERE KAREN
SOB!
LET ME HAVE A TALK WITH HIM
DID YOU LEAVE YOUR BUTTPLUG IN ALL DAY LIKE I TOLD YOU?
YES MOMMY!!

DID YOU FINISH WRITING THE CRITICAL APPRECIATION OF AUDRE LORDE'S "SISTER, OUTSIDER" THAT I ASSIGNED YOU?
YES MOMMY!!
DISGUSTING WORM
CLEAN MY BOOTS WITH YOUR TONGUE
PAY ME REPARATIONS
YES MOMMY
SWOOSH
VENMO: "MOMMY'S-CUM DUMP" PAID YOU $5000
DING
Crisco
KNOCK
KNOCK
KNOCK
DO NOT DISTURB
CBT
IN PROGRESS
I HOPE HE MEANS COGNITIVE BEHAVIOURAL THERAPY AND NOT COCK AND BALL TORTURE
HELLO SON
FUCK YOU DAD! SELFISH FUCKING NEO-CON WHITE SUPREMACIST OLIGARCH!!
SLATHER
I HOPE YOUR PLANE EXPLODES! I'LL BE PISSING ON YOUR GRAVE!
Crisco
SQUELCH
MY LAWYER SERVED YOU THE WRIT FROM MY COUNTER SUIT THIS MORNING-
YOU HAVE UNTIL TOMMOROW TO RESPOND!
SPLAT
SPLAT
SPLAT
SPLAT
NOW GET THE FUCK OUT OF MY ROOM!

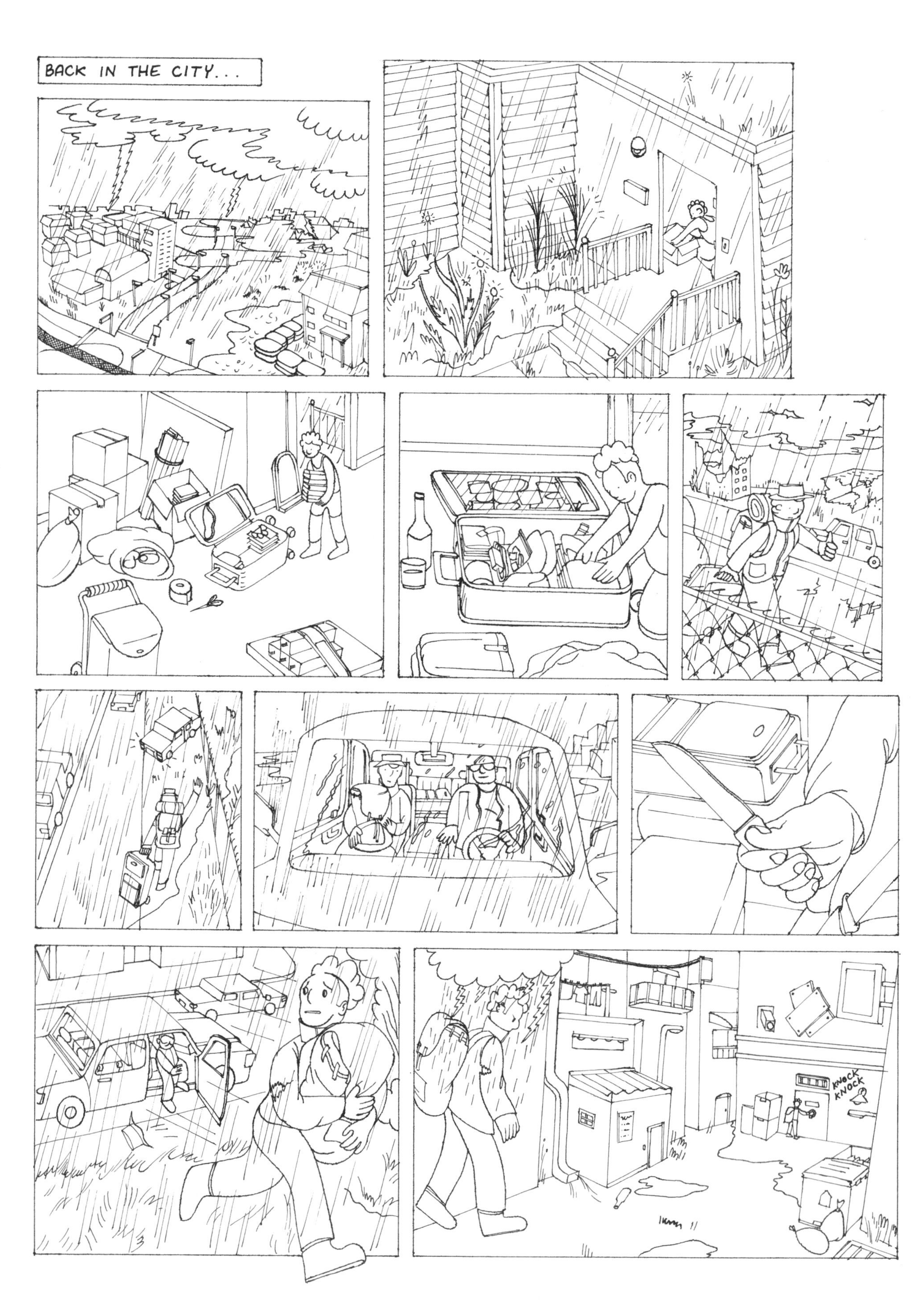
BACK IN THE CITY...
KNOCK
KNOCK

WELCOME — BEFORE WE GO ANY FURTHER
I'LL HAVE TO ASK YOU TO REMOVE TOUCH & FACIAL IDENTIFICATION FROM ALL OF YOUR DEVICES

THEN DEPOSIT THEM INTO THIS FARADAY CAGE UNTIL WE CAN JAILBREAK AND REUPLOAD THEM ONTO AN ENCRYPTED NETWORK

WE ARE THE RAINBOW COALITION, AN SJW* COLLECTIVE AND CROSS RACIAL LGBTQQIP2SAA** UNDERGROUND RESISTANCE MOVEMENT
*SOCIAL JUSTICE WARRIOR
** LESBIAN, GAY, BISEXUAL, TRANSGENDER, QUESTIONING, QUEER, INTERSEX, PANSEXUAL, 2 SPIRIT, ANDROGYNOUS, ASEXUAL

OUR GOAL IS TO DISRUPT AND ULTIMATELY DISSOLVE THE VIOLENTLY COERCIVE CORPORATE STATE

AND AWAKE THE WORLD FROM THE NIGHTMARE OF LIBERTARIAN POST-CAPITALIST FASCISM

ARE YOU INTERESTED IN LEARNING MORE?
YES!
SJW

SJW

WHIRR
RUMBLE

LET ME SHOW YOU AROUND

IN THE LATE 2020s WE TRANSITIONED FROM SOCIAL JUSTICE WARRIORS TO SOCIAL JUSTICE MURDERERS

DON'T WORRY, THE MURDER IS PURELY INTERNAL, LIKE JIHAD IS AN INTERIOR SPIRITUAL WAR

YOU KNOW- "KILL THE COP IN YOUR HEAD"

ALSO WE ADVOCATE FOR "PROPAGANDA OF THE DEED"
SO YOU'RE TERRORISTS ?

WHAT IS TERRORISM? — THE FORMER U.S.* WAS THE LARGEST EXPORTER OF WORLD TERROR IN HISTORY BUT WAS NEVER RECOGNIZED AS SUCH
* UNITED STATES

CIA* ORCHESTRATED COUPS AND MILITARY INTER-VENTION ACROSS LATIN AMERICA, AFRICA AND THE MIDDLE-EAST
* CENTRAL INTELLIGENCE AGENCY

ISN'T THE CLIMATE CRISIS INTENTIONAL & ORGANIZED VIOLENCE?
WHY IS STATE VIOLENCE CONDONED BUT SELF-LIBERATION CONDEMNED ?

AND SO:

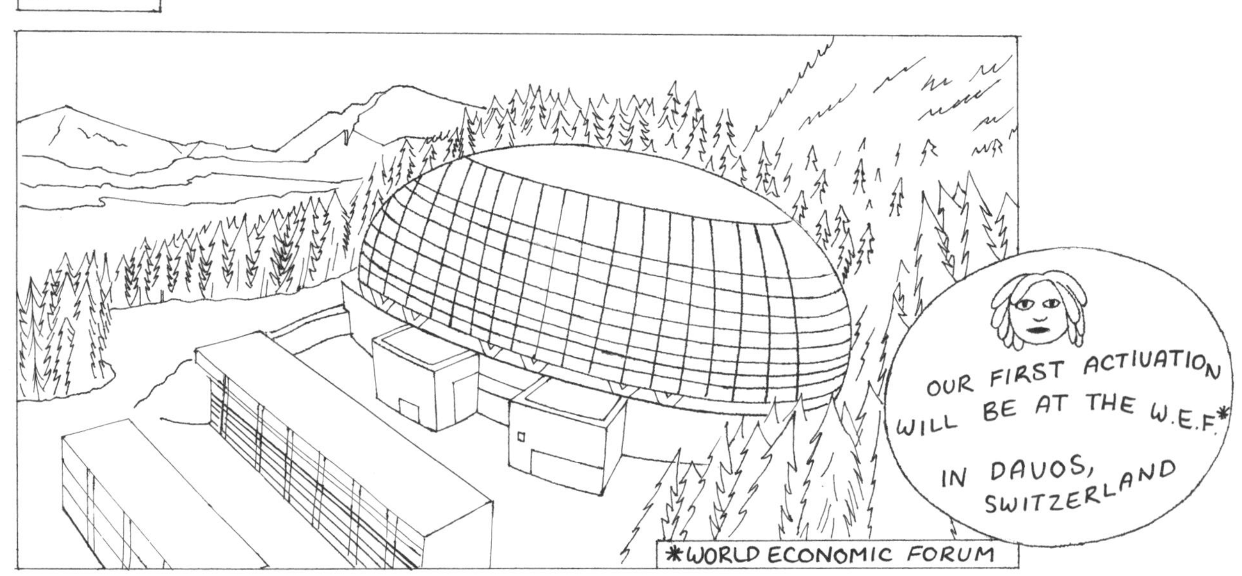
OUR FIRST ACTIVATION WILL BE AT THE W.E.F.* IN DAVOS, SWITZERLAND
*WORLD ECONOMIC FORUM

HEY SIRI, PLAY "ALL THE THINGS SHE SAID" BY t.A.T.u.
ALL THE THINGS SHE SAID
ALL THE THINGS SHE SAID
RUNNING THROUGH MY HEAD
RUNNING THROUGH MY HEAD
RUNNING THROUGH MY HEAD
ALL THE THINGS SHE S
THE EXPLOSIVE POWER OF THEIR QUEER RACIALIZED LOVE INSTANTLY DECIMATES THE CONVENTION KILLING 156 PEOPLE AND INJURING HUNDREDS MORE – THE BLAST REVERBERATES AROUND THE WORLD. IN THE COMING YEARS MANY THINGS CHANGE...
SYLVIA'S FRIEND ELEANOR FINALLY SUCCEEDS IN ORGANIZING A LABOR UNION AT EMERGENTECH AFTER SEVERAL EFFORTS ARE QUASHED BY THE GOVERNMENT IN THE NAME OF PROTECTING FINANCE CAPITAL
WE WILL FIGHT UNTIL WE WIN!
UNFORTUNATELY, ONCE THE COMPANY IS FORCED TO PAY THEIR EMPLOYEES A LIVING WAGE, REMUNERATE YEARS OF ARREARS, AND ABSORB THE COST OF THEIR ENVIRONMENTAL DAMAGE THEY BECOME FINANCIALLY INSOLVENT AND FILE FOR BANKRUPTCY
OUT OF BUSINESS

KEN'S EXTREMELY COMBATIVE AND LITIGIOUS NATURE AS A DEVELOPER EARNS HIM SO LONG A LIST OF ADVERSARIES THAT WHEN HE IS EVENTUALLY FOUND SLAIN IN HIS HOME POLICE ARE NEVER ABLE TO PENETRATE THE BYZANTINE NETWORK OF ESPIONAGE, SCANDALS AND LEGAL BATTLES HE WAS EMBROILED IN AND THE CASE REMAINS UNSOLVED.

KEN JR INHERITS HIS FATHER'S ESTATE THEN USES THE FORTUNE TO CONTINUE SOLICITING FINDOM* MARIELLE WHO EVENTUALLY ORDERS HER PAY PIG TO SURRENDER ALL OF HIS FINANCES TO ANONYMOUSLY FUNDING THE RAINBOW COALITION. ADAPTIVE REUSE HAS KEN'S FORMER MANSION CONVERTED INTO A NON-PROFIT BONG AND DILDO FACTORY DEDICATED TO SERVING THE SAME WORKING CLASS COMMUNITIES HE'D DISPLACED

* FINANCIAL DOMINATION

SYLVIA AND MARIELLE LIVE HAPPILY EVER AFTER IN AN OPEN LIFE PARTNERSHIP. THEIR POLITICAL GESTURE IGNITES A GLOBAL MOVEMENT. THROUGH A DECADES-LONG INTERNATIONAL PROGRAMME OF COORDINATED LABOR STRIKES AND VIOLENT UPRISINGS THEY ARE ABLE TO HALT GLOBAL FINANCE ENTIRELY AND SEIZE CONTROL OF THE WORLD'S GOVERNMENTS WITH THE GOAL OF PRODUCING AN EQUITABLE SOCIETY.

HUMANITY ENTERS A GOLDEN AGE OF PROSPERITY. REDISTRIBUTION OF WEALTH ON A MASSIVE SCALE ENDS HOMELESSNESS, POVERTY AND HUNGER GLOBALLY. SALARY CAPS, FREE EDUCATION, COMMUNITY CARE, TRANSFORMATIVE JUSTICE AND HORIZONTAL ORGANIZATION OF POWER ALL BECOME CORNERSTONES OF HISTORY'S FIRST TRUE DEMOCRACY. THE UTOPIAN VISION OF SOCIETY SEES ACCELERATING BREAKTHROUGHS IN THE FIELDS OF MEDICINE, TECHNOLOGY AND THE ARTS. THIS ERA LASTS FOR SEVERAL CENTURIES.

SOMEWHERE ALONG THE WAY, HOWEVER, THEIR PROJECT GOES AWRY – AND BECOMES... *REVERSE RACISM*. ALL OF WESTERN EUROPE IS ANNEXED AND DIVIDED BETWEEN NEW COLONIAL SUPER POWERS, THE COAST BORDERING THE ATLANTIC OCEAN IS RENAMED THE SLAVE COAST. BELGIUM IS GIVEN TO THE CONGO WHERE TEN MILLION BELGIANS ARE WORKED TO DEATH OR MURDERED IN ONE OF THE WORLD'S MOST DEVASTATING GENOCIDES. BRITAIN IS TURNED INTO THE BRITAIN COMPANY, JOINT OWNERSHIP OF WHICH IS SHARED BY MULTIPLE NATIONS ACROSS ASIA AND AFRICA. THE CONTENTS OF THE NATIONAL GALLERY ARE LOOTED, FARMERS ARE REQUIRED TO PRODUCE MONOCULTURES FOR EXPORT TO WEALTHIER NATIONS WHILE FAMINE RAVAGES THEIR POPULATION. AFTER SUFFERING A BRUTAL MASSACRE, WHITE PEOPLE IN THE SETTLER STATES OF AMERICA, CANADA, AUSTRALIA AND NEW ZEALAND ARE FORCIBLY REMOVED FROM THEIR HOMES AND PLACED ON SMALL PARCELS OF LAND AND INTO SPECIALIZED INSTITUTIONS IN WHICH THEY ARE TAUGHT TO SPEAK THE LANGUAGES OF INDIGENOUS COMMUNITIES AND FORBIDDEN TO SPEAK ENGLISH

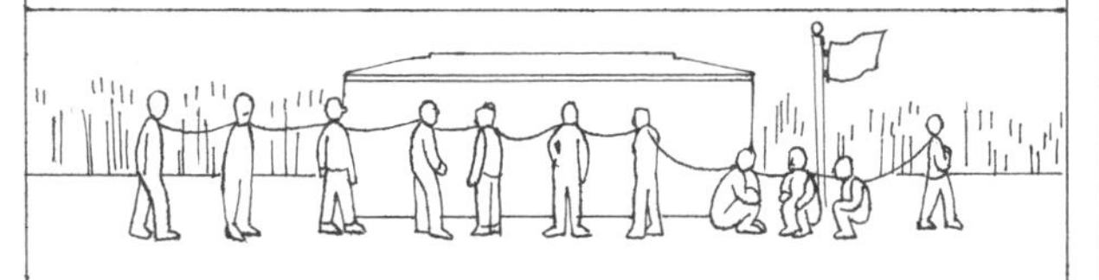

AFTER GENERATIONS OF RESISTANCE WHITE PEOPLE ARE GRANTED SOME RIGHTS. EXPLICITLY RACIST PRACTICES LIKE SLAVERY AND APARTHEID ARE ABOLISHED BUT ANTI-WHITE RACISM INSTEAD BECOMES CODIFIED INTO A SYSTEM. REPORTS OF MISSING AND MURDERED WHITE MEN ARE NEVER INVESTIGATED BY POLICE AND WHITE COMMUNITIES FACE HARSHER SENTENCING AND ARE DISPROPORTIONATELY INCARCERATED IN A PRISON SYSTEM WHICH FORCES THEM TO SUPPLY FREE LABOR. WHITE CHILDREN ARE OVER REPRESENTED IN THE CHILD WELFARE SYSTEM AND REGULARLY STOLEN FROM THEIR FAMILIES AND PUT INTO FOSTER CARE OR ADOPTION. WHITE PEOPLE ARE DENIED ACCESS TO EDUCATION, LOANS, AND HOUSING, PREVENTING THEM FROM ESTABLISHING GENERATIONAL WEALTH. INNOCENT WHITE MEN ARE INDISCRIMINATELY MURDERED BY POLICE WHO ARE NEVER HELD ACCOUNTABLE FOR THEIR EXTRAJUDICIAL KILLINGS. EUROPEAN NATIONS ARE OFFICIALLY DECLARED INDEPENDANT BUT TRIBUTE IS STILL COLLECTED FROM THEM IN THE FORM OF COERCIVE ECONOMIC RESTRUCTURING AND FOREIGN INVESTMENT AS A SUBSTITUTE FOR OCCUPATION. WHEN THE PEOPLE OF EUROPE DEMOCRATICALLY ELECT POPULISTS WHO REFUSE TO PAY THEIR COUNTRY'S UNFAIRLY IMPOSED GLOBAL DEBT, FOREIGN GOVERNMENTS CONSPIRE TO OVERTHROW THEIR NEW PRESIDENTS AND REPLACE THEM WITH LEADERS MORE SYMPATHETIC TO THEIR INTERESTS. NEWLY INDEPENDANT NATIONS ARE LEFT ROBBED OF RESOURCES WITH THEIR SOCIAL AND ECONOMIC INFRASTRUCTURE IN SHAMBLES. EUROPE BECOMES A PLAYGROUND FOR MERCENARY WARS AND DESPOTS.

THE END

THE ARTIST, SAEHMEH AEHLAWAHNI, PUTS DOWN HIS PEN AFTER INKING THE FINAL PANEL OF HIS NEWEST COMIC, "ATROCITY EXHIBITION"
WAS IT RIGHT WHAT I DID?
WAS THIS HOW THE STORY WAS SUPPOSED TO END?
I DON'T KNOW...
ALL I DID WAS DESCRIBE REAL EVENTS FROM COLONIAL HISTORY–
BUT IN REVERSE!
THE SCALE OF BARBARISM SEEMS SO UNREAL THEY CAN HARDLY BE BELIEVED
PEOPLE MIGHT ACTUALLY THINK I WANT THESE THINGS TO HAPPEN
WHEN ALL I WAS TRYING TO ILLUSTRATE IS THAT REVERSE RACISM ISN'T REAL!
AND WHAT OF MY DEPICTION OF MARIELLE?
I TRIED TO WRITE HER AS STRONG AND ARTICULATE BUT MAYBE IT'S NOT MY PLACE TO PORTRAY A SEX WORKER CHARACTER AT ALL...
I DON'T WANT TO END UP LIKE THAT RACIST LIONEL SHRIVER
MAYBE IT'S NECESSARY TO STATE WITHIN THE STORY IN SOME WAY THAT I UNEQUIVOCALLY SUPPORT SEX WORKERS IN THEIR FIGHT FOR FAIR AND SAFE WORKING CONDITIONS
FOSTA & SESTA
LATER
A FICTION IS, IN ITSELF, A STATEMENT
ONE THAT SLIPS THROUGH OUR FINGERS LIKE SAND WHEN WE TRY TO GRASP IT
WHICH IS MAYBE WHY EVEN I AM CONFUSED BY WHAT I HAVE CREATED
CLICK

ABOUT THE AUTHOR